CRITICAL ACCLAIM FOR
THE PRICE YOU PAY

"Jim Fusilli has done a lot of good writing in his time, but *The Price You Pay* is his best book. It's everything you want urban crime fiction to be: taut, seriously suspenseful, closely observed, wry, and very knowing about the way the real world works. I started off admiring the precision of the writing, and then found the pages flying. I was going to say George V. Higgins, the author of *The Friends of Eddie Coyle*, would have liked this novel. But then again, he might have just been pissed that he didn't write it himself."

—Peter Blauner, author and screenwriter

"With *The Price You Pay*, Jim Fusilli gives us a tough and heartfelt coming of age crime story—gritty, suspenseful, involving. The characters pop and ache and burn. Mickey Wright is memorable."

—Meg Gardiner, #1 *New York Times* bestselling author

CRITICAL ACCLAIM FOR JIM FUSILLI

THE PRICE YOU PAY

BOOKS BY JIM FUSILLI

Closing Time (Putnam, 2001)
A Well-Known Secret (Putnam, 2002)
Tribeca Blues (Putnam, 2003)
Hard, Hard City (Putnam, 2004)
Pet Sounds (Continuum, 2007)
Marley Z and the Blood-Stained Violin (Dutton Juvenile, 2008)
Narrows Gate (Amazon Publishing, 2011)
Road to Nowhere (Thomas & Mercer, 2012)
Billboard Man (Thomas & Mercer, 2013)
The Mayor of Polk Street (Audible, 2019)
The Price You Pay (Down & Out Books, 2024)

JIM FUSILLI

THE PRICE YOU PAY

Down & Out Books
3959 Van Dyke Road, Suite 265
Lutz, FL 33558
DownAndOutBooks.com

Cover design by Joe Dizney

ISBN: 1-64396-352-X
ISBN-13: 978-1-64396-352-5

To Terry Williams

"You make up your mind, you choose the chance you take."
—Bruce Springsteen

"Rolling in the muck is not the best way of getting clean."
—Aldous Huxley

CHAPTER ONE

Flour in the folds of his washed jeans, flour coating his white Adidas sneakers, Mickey Wright went directly from Corso's Bakery to Our Lady Queen of Martyrs for 6:30 a.m. Mass. He sat in his customary spot, a good distance from the black-veiled Polish widows and retired dock workers cragged and hunched in ill-fitting clothes and well-shined shoes. Creeping above the Manhattan skyline, peeking between the newly completed World Trade Center towers, the sun pushed its light through the arched stained-glass windows of the old gray stone church. Less than a city block away, the Hudson splashed against rotting piers. In his pew, Mickey could smell the fetid river. He heard seagulls caw.

A graduate of nearby St. Peter's Prep, Mickey was the youngest member of the congregation of the last church in Jersey City to say Sunday Mass in Latin. He came to Queen of Martyrs as part of a tradition unrelated to language: It had been his late mother's parish as a child and throughout her life, cut short by cancer. The loss had devastated him. They were alike, Mickey and his mother, as his father would point out, often angrily as if their shared personalities were deficient. Quiet, guarded, inconspicuous, friendly but slow to make friends, they preferred their own company and the company of each other, Dotty, who read newspapers from front to back, Mickey a boy with his toy soldiers, Lincoln Logs and Saturday morning

3

cartoons. Mickey remembered with cinematic clarity his mother on the hunt for bargains, rummaging through the racks at S. Klein, Korvetts, Two Guys and other discount department stores a bus ride away from their walk-up in the Heights, Mickey waiting patiently as she held up shirts and jeans to gauge their fit, the clothes always a bit too large so they might last more than a season. Shopping done, they would have lunch together at a Chinese restaurant in Journal Square, sharing shrimp chow mein and white rice. Smoking had dulled his mother's taste buds, so she was an indifferent eater and a less-than-mediocre cook—her chicken dry, beef gray and bloodless, vegetables as flavorless as their cardboard packaging—but she did relish her lunches at the Canton Tea Garden with her son. She would coo when the waiter lifted the serving platter's silver dome.

Mickey had his mother's pale blue eyes, which gave him the appearance of someone inattentive or lost to his own thoughts. Whereas Dotty Wright was stout and rubbery, Mickey was lean and sinewy, long-legged as was his sister Rosemary. Pleasantly featured, he parted in his brown hair in the middle and wore sideburns in the style of the day. He had the kind of skin that tanned easily. This morning, as the bright July sun promised a scorching day, he thought of his mother slathering on suntan lotion during their annual summer week down at Ideal Beach, desperate for her skin to take on a glow. "You're turning orange, Ma," said Rosemary, who freckled wildly.

Given his older sister had fled Jersey City at age 16, memories of Dotty were Mickey's sole link to the warmth of family. In his darker moments, he considered himself an orphan, though his father was still the dominant living figure in his life. Prior to his mother's death, Mickey's biggest disappointment had been the realization his father was a fraud. He came to that conclusion when he was eight, unaware it was the consensus in the Heights, if not the entire city. "He's a douchebag. An asshole," Rosemary told him, her cheek still bearing the red print of their father's palm.

Seeking peace, young Mickey defended the indefensible, "I bet a lot of cops seem like assholes."

"He's a special kind of asshole," Rosemary replied. "Oh, our Pop. He's a one-in-a-million asshole."

In the early morning, Queen of Martyrs was cool, its white interior walls immune to humidity and oppressive heat. As Mickey settled in, the mournful sound of a pipe organ wafted from the choir loft. The solemn music and the tranquil ambiance ushered him into a sort of trance, his loneliness allayed by a temporary sense of belonging, of acceptance and approval. With little difficulty, he conjured his mother, who prayed with fervor, rosary beads wrapped around her shopworn hands.

Deep in his peace, he was unaware a man now stood next to him.

"Michael Wright Jr.," hiss-whispered the church's handyman.

Mickey turned slowly. "Wiktor."

"Father Stan needs you, Michael Wright Jr. The altar boy, he's not here."

Mickey looked at his watch. "He'll be here. Don't worry."

"Father Stan needs you. The altar boy, he's not here," repeated Wiktor, who had taken shrapnel to the side of his head during World War II. He was on the verge of panic, his assignment incomplete.

"OK, OK," said Mickey, as he slid out of his pew. He followed Wiktor to the sacristy. Soon he was wearing the handyman's shoes and a pair of the priest's black socks. The surplice was snug, the black cassock just about covered his jeans. Wiktor had already prepared the altar, so there was little to do.

His accent betraying his Szczecin roots, Father Stanislaus, in full vestments, thanked Mickey, lifted his chalice and nodded it was time for Mass to begin. Wiktor pulled back the door and Mickey led the priest from the sacristy toward the altar.

The parishioners rose in unison.

"*In nómine Patris, et Fíliii, et Spíritus Sancti*," Father Stan intoned.

"Amen," said Mickey, who first served Mass at age seven. "*Dóminus vobíscum.*"

"*Et cum spíritu tuo,*" he replied.

Continuing in Latin, the priest invited the congregation to acknowledge their sins.

As did Mickey, they responded: "*Mea culpa, mea culpa, mea máxima culpa.*"

Mickey left through the church rather than the sacristy, stopping for a moment of private prayer as he lit a candle. When he exited, he found his father leaning against his squad car, arms folded, glowering with impatience.

"Where the fuck have you been?" said Mike Wright, in his Jersey City Police Department blues, his eight-point hat and nightstick elsewhere, his sidearm in its holster.

"The altar boy didn't show," Mickey shrugged.

"A 20-year-old altar boy. Jesus. That's you right there."

Mike Wright was a bit shorter than his son, and a paunch hung over his belt. His shoulders were broad, his arms brawny, his hands blunt and capable of a vise-like grips and sledgehammer blows. His hair had thinned considerable and his nose bore the signs of having been broken while he was in the Marines, serving stateside as an MP during the Korean conflict. Early on, a partner said Wright was built like a tombstone with a face; he and his son shared no resemblance. Dotty Wright had thought of him as ruggedly handsome. She said he was a good dancer.

"Everything all right?" said Mickey as he approached his father.

During the endless summer of '67, when race riots consumed nearby Newark, Mike Wright shot and killed a black man, claiming he interrupted a domestic dispute during which the deceased was beating his wife with a bicycle chain. A protest ensued: TV crews from across the river attended a march toward City Hall, broadcasting about 100 people who chanted, pumped fists, held high their signs accusing the Jersey City cops of callous disregard for black lives. Violence was expected, so Mike shooed Dotty and the kids down the shore. When they returned, they couldn't escape the echo of condemnation. As if in anticipation, Rosemary had called her father a killer on the bus ride north from Ideal Beach. Mickey felt accused. He entered St. Peter's Prep under a cloud. Dotty prayed.

The widow sued the city and received a six-figure settlement. Wright's career was curtailed, JCPD succumbing to political pressure. They shuttled him among a variety of paper-pushing assignments he considered insulting. But in January, some five years after the incident, Wright received a reprieve, its source a mystery to Mickey, whose communication with his father was limited to necessity and terse responses to his provocations. Wright now patrolled the housing projects that dotted Jersey City, giving him latitude and discretion. Mickey saw his father's swagger return, his grievances diminish. But he suspected he hadn't fully escaped the shadows. When the phone rang, Wright hurried to the kitchen to answer it. His replies were brief: "Yeah," "sure," "no problem." Then he would exit in civilian clothes, his firearm in its shoulder holster.

"You. You're with me," Wright said now, facing the Queen of Martyr's façade. Without further word, he walked around the front of the squad car and slid behind the wheel. He reached over and flung open the passenger's side door.

Mickey stuck in his head. "Where are we going?"

"Get in."

Wright put his hat on the console. A shotgun was locked in place, its barrel pointed toward the navy-and-white Fury's roof.

When his son closed the door, Wright roared the car from the curb.

"Where are we going?" Mickey repeated.

"I got you a job. And you're gonna take it."

Wright punched the siren and drove through the red light at Montgomery Street.

7

"I've got a job," Mickey told him. "Two. I've got two jobs."

Wright took a hard right onto the boulevard. "You got no jobs. Zero jobs. You're a delivery boy at a shit-stain liquor store and you hang out at a bakery that has to give its bread away."

Only half true. Frank's Liquors was a dump, but Corso's donated its bread because it went stale if it wasn't eaten within 24 hours, its 100-year-old recipe swearing off eggs and preservatives, using only water, flour, yeast and salt. Most days, Corso's shut down early, its Italian loafs, flat bread and high rounds baked on the premises all sold. If there were leftovers, Sammy Corso let the poor come by and take away a loaf or two, no charge.

"You're not a baker."

"No, not yet. But I'm learning."

"And you're not a Corso. If you think the guineas will let you in, you're out of your mind." Wright shook his head. "Standing around from four in the morning, watching them make bread. Jesus."

"An apprentice. It's good work. It takes skill."

Raising his voice, Mike Wright said, "Listen to me: You're going to take this fuckin' job."

Though the siren was silent, cars moved aside as the cherry-top Fury turned toward the Holland Tunnel, its tires squealing.

"In New York?" Mickey asked.

"No. We're going to the All-Star."

A diner on the north side of the access road. Wright came to the traffic light and made a U-turn, cutting off traffic heading west to the skyway.

"You're going to talk to Mr. Swayback. You answer his questions, and you thank him. You don't make a fuckin' monkey out of yourself, and you're pulling down eight bucks an hour."

"Doing what?"

"Office work. You type. Whatever."

Eight dollars an hour, thought Mickey Wright. He was making $1.75 plus tips at Frank's. Corso's was paying him in knowledge and fresh bread.

"Edward Swayback? The councilman?"

"Impact is in his ward. Impact Trucking and Transport. If Eddie says OK, then tomorrow you go see Joe DeSalvo, the union rep. The Teamsters. If you don't fuck up, you start right away."

The Fury thudded into the parking lot.

"What about school? I'll have classes—"

"It's four to midnight."

Wright jerked the car into park and cut the engine. "I pulled a lot of strings to set this up. When Eddie talks to you, you answer," he told his son. "Don't sit there, a fuckin' clam like your mother."

Then he said, "Let's go."

They entered the diner slowly, tentatively, which surprised Mickey. His father usually barreled into rooms, aiming to take possession with his presence and a gunfighter's stance. At the cashier's station, little mints and a spoon in a plate, Mickey watched as Wright spotted the councilman in a booth in a back corner. He whacked Mickey with the back of his hand, an annoyance since childhood.

"Hold on," said Wright, gesturing with his chin. "He's with somebody."

A man in a black vest and white shirt, menus in hand, approached. "Officer, just two?"

"Coffee black. To go," Wright replied, holding up a lone finger. "One."

Pies rotated inside a glass case. Dishes clattered. Mickey heard a spatula chopping against a griddle, he smelled frying onions. A waitress walked by, balancing three coffee cups. Wright stood with his feet spread, hand resting on his sidearm.

In back, the woman who had been sitting across from Swayback wriggled out of the booth. Mickey watched. She said something. He smiled without warmth. In her 40s, wearing a short floral dress and sandals, she walked along the aisle as if relieved, color returning to her face.

"Mrs. Swayback," said Mike Wright with a nod.

Clutching a white purse, she looked into Mickey's pale blue eyes, but moved quickly without a word or acknowledgment. Mickey thought her attractive for her age, busty and tempting, with an air of something concealed, though he may have misread her completely. With women, Mickey's inexperience was profound. He had the pure, hopeful heart of the unaware.

Swayback beckoned them with a little gesture.

"Come on," said Wright.

They passed occupied stools and booths.

Swayback didn't stand.

"Eddie, this is my son, Mickey."

"The St. Peter's boy," said Swayback. He had been picking at eggs, bacon, white toast. "Sit."

"Go ahead," Wright said. To Swayback, he added, "I'll let you be. Hey, thanks again, Eddie."

Swayback nodded, his eyes on Mickey as he slipped into the booth.

"Coffee?"

"No thank you, sir," Mickey said.

Swayback was about his father's age, with a full head of graying hair, meticulously styled, razor cut; square jawed, he was fit and robust. To Mickey, he seemed vaguely threatening and yet somewhat amused.

"You're interested in Impact," said Swayback, who wore a blue golf shirt, a thin gold watch and a wedding band.

Mickey Wright understood how transactions with authority should transpire. Nuns and Jesuits had educated him. Politeness had long served him well.

"I am interested, sir."

"What kind of skills do you have?"

"I can type fairly well," Mickey said. "I'm organized. I work hard."

"You're working now?"

Mickey nodded. "Frank's Liquors on Summit. I started in high school."

Swayback knew this was so. He also knew Frank Zerline had run up $400 in parking tickets he wanted wiped away and his wife had been picked up in North Bergen with a vial of illegal German diet pills. Taking from Zerline posed no threat.

"He'll miss you?"

"I can't say," Mickey replied, "but I am reliable."

Yeah, fuck Zerline, thought Swayback. "Impact is a big operation. I like to see people from our ward inside the place."

"Yes, sir."

"Do you know Joe DeSalvo?"

"He sponsors a Little League team."

"Benny Luna?"

"No, sir."

Swayback said, "He's the dock boss. Good man. One of us."

A waitress arrived the fresh coffee. It steamed as she refilled his cup.

"What about your studies?" Swayback said as he took a careful sip.

"If we begin at four, I can adjust my classes in the Fall."

"Good," Swayback said. "How's Father Angelini?"

The president of St. Peter's College. "I don't know, sir."

"I'll tell him you said hi." Swayback laughed. "Go do a good job and make us proud."

They shook hands.

"Thank you for the opportunity, sir."

"Tell your father I want to see him."

Mickey did so.

He waited outside as cars traveled to and from New York, sunlight streaking the blacktop. Across the road, Exxon was selling unleaded for thirty-eight cents a gallon, a threatened jump due to an Arab oil embargo not yet in effect. Zerline gave Mickey a dollar now and then to cover his expenses for the occasional drive to the flop motels down on Tonnelle Avenue. At eight dollars an hour at Impact, Mickey wouldn't be wanting for gas money. At eight dollars an hour, Mickey Wright could put together a bankroll to get him out of here.

CHAPTER TWO

The Teamsters' offices were in neighboring Union City, a straight drive north past a reservoir and tilting homes clad in aluminum. Coming directly from the library, Mickey arrived well before his mid-afternoon appointment, finding a spot for his 1969 Chevy Impala at a meter in front of the beige-brick building. Upstairs, he was told to sit and wait.

He had expected more. In Washington, the Teamsters had a mighty office complex that overlooked the nation's capital, according to *Life*. The Union City headquarters were functional at best, outdated, almost shabby, though the vice president was considered a powerful force within the labor movement (and rumored to be associated with the Genovese crime family). Mickey waited in a small, boxy room; old magazines lay in disarray on the table set on orange shag carpeting. A floor-stand ashtray overflowed with cigarette butts. A painted portrait of Jimmy Hoffa hung on a wall covered with wood paneling; next to it was another portrait of a man who wore a worrisome frown behind eyeglasses. A lone secretary manipulated a manual typewriter with blinding speed, its clack and rattle drowning out the blather of an all-news radio station. As Mickey picked microscopic and perhaps non-existent pieces of lint from his suit slacks, the water cooler burped.

"He won't be much longer," said the secretary, a petite Cuban woman with oil-black eyes.

Mickey studied the wood paneling. The blinds were opened, but uneven, the office lit by jagged sunlight.

Soon, the secretary's phone buzzed, and she told Mickey he could see Mr. DeSalvo now.

DeSalvo was standing behind his desk, its blotter covered in open ledgers and loose documents. On the low cabinet behind him were more papers, stacked haphazardly, and gold-plated trophies, all of which bore the Teamsters' logo of a wheel with two horses' heads above it. His ruddy face long and lean, DeSalvo nodded to a chair as he dragged a comb through his hair and then his sideburns.

Mickey detected the scent of aftershave. Over the window air conditioner's wheeze, he heard the bleat of traffic down below.

"Remind me," DeSalvo said, returning the comb to the pocket of his white short-sleeved shirt.

"Michael Wright Jr. Mickey."

"The cop's kid."

Mickey nodded.

"Impact."

Again, Mickey nodded.

"What do you know about us?"

"The Teamsters are the most influential union in the country."

DeSalvo leaned on his fists. "Our local—10,000 members at 400 companies in the metropolitan area. Nothing moves in or out without us. Understand?"

"Yes I do," Mickey replied.

"Nothing and nobody is bigger than the union. Everybody gets along, everything runs smooth. Your father tell you?"

He hadn't, but Mickey said, "Yes sir."

"A machine. You don't forget that."

DeSalvo reached for his pack of Parliament cigarettes. He offered one to Mickey, who declined and waited as the union boss sparked a grenade-sized lighter.

"What goes on is our business, nobody else's. You hear me?"

"I do."

"You got a problem, you see Benny Luna."

"The dock boss." Mickey understood the clerical job was his.

DeSalvo issued a plume of smoke. "It don't matter you work in the office. Benny is our guy. You're our guy. Everybody gets along. A machine.

"This is why the office personnel at Impact is ours now," he continued. "Because everybody gets along. You think, I work in the office, I'm management. You're not management. You're one of us. Ten thousand strong. *Capisce?*"

"Yes, sir."

"Give me an hour to call Benny. He'll set you up. Broadhead is the office manager, but Benny will set you up."

"Thank you, Mr. DeSalvo."

"Tell your old man. He wants to thank Swayback, fine. He should."

"I will."

They shook hands.

DeSalvo said, "You got ten thousand brothers now, kid. They got your back, and they won't bend, they don't break."

Mickey thanked him again. DeSalvo pointed to the door.

Impact was situated under the Pulaski Skyway, a dark, rusty, steel-truss bridge not a far ride from St. Peter's College; the trucking company was cloaked in streaks of shadows even on the brightest days. Drawing near on his drive from the Heights, Mickey was jostled by potholes, then greeted by the odor of gasoline and motor oil and the sound of grinding gears and barking men. He watched as incoming trucks, their steel-gray bodies sullied with grime, zipped in backwards to their stations while the long semis required pinpoint dance-like maneuvers to precisely position them for loading. All but the containers bore the Impact logo—a boxing glove landing a crushing blow, causing stars to shoot, fireworks to explode. When the street cleared of jockeying trucks, Mickey entered the employee parking lot and found a spot. Many of the truckers' cars wore a Teamster bumper sticker or the union's logo on the rear window.

He climbed the concrete steps to the Impact dock; it was at least as long as a football field. Toward its center, standing outside a slapdash shack, was a short, stocky Italian in his 50s, bifocals, pencil behind his ear, a shock of gray hair. As Mickey walked toward him, he noticed a Teamster pin above the brim of his well-worn black cap.

"Mr. Luna?" Mickey introduced himself.

Luna was purposeful, but not unpleasant. There was a trace of an accent in his gravel voice, and he spoke without inflection. Pointing to the far end of the long dock with his clipboard, he walked Mickey to the first of 18 ports for trucks and, as they passed stationary forklifts, hand trucks and dollies, explained the operation. The freight comes in through the piers in Brooklyn, Elizabeth, Hoboken, mostly, Luna said, and gets transferred to trucks heading to Canada. Freight coming down from Canada gets transferred for delivery throughout the tri-state area. The big firms up north trust Impact—Bombardier, Weston, Magna, Canadian Tire…The operation ran tight both ways.

"Have you ever been to Canada?" Mickey asked.

"What for?" the dock boss replied.

By now, the four-to-midnight crew began to arrive. They dressed for labor, the younger men in T-shirts and jeans, the others in loose-fitting sweatshirts and slacks, all wearing heavy boots and carrying work gloves. Mickey looked down at his blue button-down khakis and dress shoes.

"You seen Broadhead?"

Mickey said no, he hadn't.

Luna gestured with a snap of his chin.

Mickey turned toward the office, its windows above the steps to the dock.

"You punch in yet?"

No.

"Always punch in." Then he said, "Go ahead. You'll be alright."

Pasty and portly, left eye off center, hairline in full retreat, seated upright in a blazer, vest and tie, Robert Broadhead explained in flat, joyless tones: There was the daytime office upstairs. This is the night office. Duties are separate. My job is to determine the charges. The person in your job routes the freight and types the manifest; hence, Router-Typist. That big three-ring binder is the routing book. You sit at that desk there and look up most efficient point of entry to Canada. Then, after I determine the charges, you go over there and type up the manifest—

At that moment, a plastic tube rattled through an overhead pipe and landed with a thud in a wire basket between the old wooden desks. A grubby little pillow softened the blow, but not by much.

Broadhead continued. Open the tube, he said. Take out the paperwork.

Mickey examined the document, tattered and coffee-stained. Parts for roller bearings were heading to London, Ontario.

That tells you the freight's final destination. After you type the manifest, you put it back in the tube and send it out to Benny on the dock. The golden-rod copy stays here. The rest goes out there. That is the job of Router-Typist.

And that, added Broadhead, is Mrs. Ada.

Mickey had already noticed the hunched senior at the office's lone typewriter.

"Hello," he said.

She forced a smile and returned to the magazine that rested on the red Selectric.

On occasion, freight arrives early, Broadhead continued. Mrs. Ada handles the typing.

Then he told Mickey to go upstairs to Miss Murphy in

17

Personnel.

Upstairs, Mickey saw four people, including two men in short sleeves who worked adding machines. A hulking linebacker was in his office, dictating to a busty woman in a short, glove-tight dress. Mickey would soon be told he was Vince Miglio, Impact's general manager, and she was Louise, his secretary. No one paid Mickey any mind as he proceeded, hesitantly, around a corner where he found Miss Murphy in a boxy little room.

"Michael Wright Jr.," she said with a smile when Mickey tapped on her door frame. "Come in." In her 40s, she wore her hair in a bygone style that spiraled upward like soft ice cream. As he sat, Mickey discovered she had an unfortunate body odor clouds of perfume couldn't disguise.

His W-4s and forms for Social Security and pension completed, the company's vacation policy explained, Mickey returned to the night office. As soon as he entered, Mrs. Ada began packing her tote, collecting her framed photos of her grandchildren, her artificial roses in a ceramic vase, her coffee mug, a Tupperware container that held her molasses-flavored candy.

He noticed two rectangular forms, its many pages separated by carbon paper, set in an in-box next to the electric typewriter. As Mrs. Ada exited with a vague "good night," Mickey asked Broadhead if he needed to send the forms out to Luna.

Of course, Broadhead replied. He repeated earlier instructions: Pull the carbon paper, keep the golden-rod copy, put the remaining pages in a tube. Send.

As if anticipating Mickey's question, Broadhead added, Drop the carbon paper on the floor. Sweep up after I leave.

Mickey soon learned the job required more than the tasks Broadhead described. Each night, he was responsible for the lunch run—lunch time being at about 8 p.m. on the four-to-midnight shift. Most men brought food from home, as a cost-savings measure and, as Mickey witnessed, a means to a quality meal for the dock workers whose wives or mothers cooked like masters. Others, mostly the single men or widowers, sent out for their food. Well before Mickey was hired, Broadhead had agreed to an arrangement: So that the full crew could keep working, the Router-Typist would drive to the White Mana, Chicken Delight or Monteleone's sandwich shop in Journal Square to pick up an order he'd call in. Mickey would deliver the food to an old wooden cable reel near Luna's shack, the door boss would blow the horn and the crew picked up their meals, eating on discarded crates or seated on a forklift. A few retreated to the break room under the day office; designated for the Canadian drivers waiting to return toward home, it was kept clean, as was the locker room next door. Preferring his own company, Broadhead ate his brown-bag sandwiches in his car while he did the crossword puzzle in ink under the dome light. Since Broadhead had kept working while Mickey was gone, a pile of bills of lading awaited his return.

Part of the agreement was Mickey's nightly meal was paid for by the dock workers as sort of a tip. The system was based on trust, the guys tossing into a pot—a shabby manila envelope in Luna's booth. If the pot ran low, Mickey covered the shortage himself, paying out of pocket for a burger or an overstuffed sandwich smothered in hot peppers. He didn't mind. By now, the crew treated him like he belonged. He had given up the preppy apparel.

One steamy evening, as he walked back to the office, his sandwich wrapped in butcher paper, Carl Janowitz intercepted him. Carl offered Mickey a smoke, a common courtesy. When Mickey declined, Jano lit one for himself. "It's Bippo stiffing you."

Dominick Bippo: beady-eyed, wiry, fidgety under a greasy shirt and ill-fitting jeans. Mickey noticed the rest of the dock crew treated him like a troublesome pet.

Jano dipped into his pocket and produced a $20 bill.

"Take it," he said. He was a big man, big hands.

19

Mickey shook his head. "No, no. We're square, Jano," he told him.

"Go ahead," Jano insisted, pushing the bill into Mickey's palm. "I'll get it back. Bippo won't fuck with me."

Reluctantly, Mickey agreed. Jano had status among the workers. He carried himself right.

"You going back to college?" he asked.

Mickey nodded. "Monday, in fact."

"St. Peter's, right? What's it like?"

"Like high school with more choices. I mean, I've got a locker. No dorms."

"Not like in the movies," Jano said.

Mickey said no, not like in the movies.

"You're not tempted to quit? You're making good money. The Teamsters." Then Jano clapped him on the arm. "Anybody fucks with you, you see me."

He walked off, slaloming around stacked pallets and loose freight.

With classes underway—on Mondays and Thursdays, his first was at 8 a.m.—and Impact keeping him up well past midnight, Mickey dragged for much for the week. To satisfy his major, he was required to take such courses as Forensic Accounting, Uniform Commercial Code and Macroeconomic Principles. His electives included American Lit and Geology. That full course load filled his daily schedule; in essence, he was at full speed from seven o'clock wakeup until he fell into bed eighteen hours later. He had to struggle to stay awake during Geology, a class he took only because it fit a hole in his calendar.

When the bell rang after one grindingly tedious session, an auburn-haired girl, plump and pretty, who sat across from him asked, "What are we doing here?"

Mickey said, "Penance?"

Debbie Olsen smiled. "Me, I don't know a stalagmite from a

stalactite."

"One goes up, the other goes down."

"Which is which?" They walked toward the classroom door.

Mickey shrugged.

The need for sleep required a compromise, and for Mickey, it came with a sacrifice. No longer could he wake up well before dawn and visit Corso's Bakery run by Sammy Corso with his son and his nephew, both named Anthony, the nephew called Too. Once the shop opened, Sammy's wife Mitz worked the counter with Too, who was as affable as Anthony was stern. A first-generation immigrant from Sardinia, Sammy was lanky with Dean Martin-style salt-and-pepper hair, and he ran the bakery with casual authority. With his mother, Mickey had shopped at Corso's for as long as he could remember. They were good neighbors, the shop a jovial, no-nonsense place, and their fresh bread made Dotty's cooking nearly bearable. When he asked Sammy if he could observe their bread process, he agreed, but only after a moment's thought.

"What's your father say?" Sammy asked.

"I—I didn't tell him."

"I'm not looking for trouble."

"Me neither."

Sammy continued to ponder. "OK, then…"

The experiment began shortly after Mickey graduated from St. Peter's Prep. For weeks, he did nothing but observe, Sammy and Too explaining, Anthony annoyed by his presence, telling him to go be useful—Windex the display cases, sweep the floor, pop the dents out of the trash cans. Mickey found comfort in the reliability of their routine and purity of their mission: They woke up, they came to the shop, they made bread, they sold bread, customers went away happy and the Corsos did it again seven days a week. Even before they let him so much as carry a sack of flour, the Corsos put Mickey to work behind the counter when Mitz caught a flu. Too bagged the bread while Mickey made change, counting out coins, the little bell above the door ringing when a new customer arrived, most of whom Mickey knew by name. With little imagination, he could picture his mother coming in, ordering pizza breads, making sandwiches for her two kids and her husband, Dotty indulging in the guilty pleasure of plucking out the loaves' fluffy insides and nibbling away as she flitted around the Wrights' kitchen, the radio atop the refrigerator playing the hits of her youth.

Shortly after his mother's death, Mickey knew he would have to escape Jersey City. Not banished as Rosemary had been, but on his own terms, his contract fulfilled by graduating from the college his father had chosen and was paying for. There was nothing binding him to the Heights. Accounting would provide a transferable trade; at St. Peter's Prep, Father McInnis suggested it as a career for Mickey, who was good at math and well organized. Somewhere—the exact location never coalescing in his young mind—he would be CPA who served local commercial businesses, a contented man in a jacket and tie who provided a service in a small town where he was welcomed and appreciated.

But working at Corso's had encouraged him to consider amending his strategy: He could become a baker who managed his own books, serving excellent product for a profit. He saw a shop on Main Street somewhere that ran so efficiently he could expand his operation—one shop at the north end of the long, busy street, the other at the south end. He considered an innovation: He would deliver fresh bread to his customers. A second shift late in the day would allow bread straight from the oven to arrive at home in time for dinner.

Jesus, thought Mickey, who was blowing through life like tumbleweed, *I have options. If I break free of my old man, I can do something by choice.*

But since college resumed, Mickey had been to Corso's only once—on a Monday morning after a weekend of sound sleep and a soothing visit to Queen of Martyrs. He was standing in front of the bakery when Sammy arrived.

Sammy said, "Hey Mickey, *come va?*"

They shook hands.

Then Too came around the corner, already all in white like his uncle.

Another handshake. More good cheer.

Too said, "I hear you're doing good. Impact, right? A big outfit."

Sammy put his lunchbox under his arm to unlock the door. He said, "But your sneakers. They're filthy."

"No, it's from carbon paper. If you want, I'll take them off."

Sammy gave him an affectionate tap on the back of the head. "Go put on the coffee," he told him. Passing the display cases and the cash register, its drawer open and empty, they walked through darkness into the back room where the bread was made since the late 1940s.

Over at the sink, Mickey scrubbed up to his elbows.

Anthony arrived. Ant-knee. A permanent frown, a witch's nose. All business.

Sammy was folding a sheet from yesterday's *Jersey Journal* to make himself a hat. "Look who came home."

"Put on the radio," Anthony told Mickey. He went deep into the back room and soon he appeared in white. His father handed him a newspaper hat.

Too hauled a 25-pound bag of unbleached white flour to a table.

Anthony fired up the oven, then walked over to Mickey. "Tell me you ain't quit college."

"No," Mickey said quickly. "I was up early. That's all."

Classical music filled the backroom, something sweet but with muscle. Sammy hummed along as he unpacked the yeast.

The spiral mixer let out a groan when Too flipped the switch.

"Windex the display cases," Anthony told Mickey, nodding toward the front of the shop. "No streaks."

"No," Sammy shouted, "let him mix the dough with your cousin. Let's see what he's got."

"All right," Anthony said, not too pleased. "Then do the cases."

Mickey brought a mug of steaming coffee to Too. There were two old bowls on the table, one to scale the flour for small batches, the other for water.

"Go ahead," Too said between cautious sips. "You know what you're doing."

The sack of flour stood upright. Mickey tugged on the string to open it. The thin white cloud rose toward his face.

"So far, so good," said Too.

CHAPTER THREE

One late afternoon, Joey Baldessaro Jr., a Jersey City-based driver, pulled Mickey aside. He said, "Listen, if my wife calls, you tell her I ain't in yet."

Baldessaro was in his early 30s; like most of the drivers, he was fit and rough around the edges, but he had a kind of charm and an easy laugh. His father was a driver too; Joey Sr. gave his son his good looks but was taciturn and often abrupt. It was said both men had quick tempers

"What?" Joey Jr. said.

"I'm not comfortable with that," Mickey told him.

They were in the corridor by the time clock. Behind Joey Jr., the dock hummed with activity. It was coming up on five o'clock and many drivers had already punched out.

"Yeah, well," Joey Jr. said. "Pretend."

Soon, many of the Jersey City-based drivers counted on him for cover. "He's not in yet, Mrs. Flannery," Mickey said when she called looking for her husband, though Flannery dumped his load three hours ago. He lied to Tommy Malzone's daughter, telling her he wasn't sure where her father was when he knew Malzone was buying rounds and growing sloppy at Rudy's, spending cash he won when he hit the number. Finally, someone said it to Mickey Wright: "You're a goddamned liar!" shouted Mrs. Riccardi. "His car is in front of her house!"

"I didn't see—"

"You're a goddamned fuckin' liar" she repeated before slamming down the handset.

One night, well after the drivers were all in, Mickey answered the phone. Broadhead stared at him, as if Mickey were to blame that it rang.

It was Cheryl Peck. Her husband's father had a stroke. They took him to Christ Hospital. Do you know where he is?

Mickey said, "Let me see if I can track him down."

Buddy Peck was one of the drivers who repaired to Rudy's after he clocked out.

"I've got to go find Peck," Mickey explained to Broadhead, who clucked in annoyance. Mickey trotted through a light rain to his old Impala.

The bar was crowded, every stool filled and men leaning in between. The jukebox was blaring Creedence, drowning out the TV. Mickey looked through the haze of smoke and found Peck near the taps, a beer and an empty shot glass in front of him. He had Tommy Malzone on one side, Freddy Flannery on the other. Joey Baldessario Jr. was at the pinball machine, longneck bottle and quarters near his elbow.

Mickey entered sideways, careful not to bump men with drinks in their hands. When Malzone saw him, he let out a cheer. "College Boy!"

Peck and Flannery turned.

"Give the kid a drink," Malzone shouted to the bartender.

"No thanks, Tommy," Mickey said. "I got to get back."

"Bullshit," Malzone said. "Hang."

"Buddy, I've got to talk to you."

Peck read Mickey's expression: Something was wrong.

Mickey put his hand on Peck's shoulder, his lips near his ear.

Peck hopped off the stool.

"Christ Hospital," Mickey added.

Leaving a dollar and change on the bar, Peck bolted.

"What happened?" Flannery asked.

Mickey explained.

Tipsy, Malzone wasn't listening. He grabbed Peck's Pilsner glass and crammed it into Mickey's hand.

"Drink up," he said.

Flannery said, "I should go with him. I know Cheryl since grade school."

Mickey tried to shake free of Malzone's grip.

"Tommy," said Flannery, "leave the kid be, huh?"

"One drink. College Boy."

"Tommy..."

Mickey yanked his arm just as Malzone let go. The beer splashed from the glass onto a guy who was standing behind them.

Swearing, scowling, the guy, big and wide, grabbed Mickey by the shirtfront. He slammed him against Peck's empty chair, bruising his back.

"Whoa, bud," said Flannery. "It was an accident. Don't get all—"

"Fuck you too," the barrel-chested guy told him.

Still holding onto Mickey, the guy cocked his fist.

Joey Baldessaro Jr. hit him across the face with a beer bottle. When the guy stumbled back, blood pouring from his nose, Baldessaro pushed the broken bottle toward his chin.

By now, Flannery had joined in. He grabbed the guy by the hair and ear and tugged him to the bar. He punched his neck, the side of his head, again and again.

"Fuck who?" Flannery shouted. "Fuck me?"

The guy tried to hold up his hands in surrender.

Malzone spit at him.

"Let him go," Baldessaro said. "I'm slicing him open."

"Fellas, fellas, fellas," shouted the bartender, who raised up a baseball bat.

When Flannery shoved the guy, Baldessaro's jagged bottle slashed across his chin.

"Go ahead," Baldessaro told him. "Come back with your fuckin' army. We'll be waiting."

The guy brought his hand to his bloody nose. He looked at Mickey and stumbled away, bouncing against the men at the bar who had witnessed his defeat.

Mickey was shaking. He had beer on his jeans, blood on his gray T.

Baldessaro put the broken bottle on the bar. "You OK?"

Mickey nodded blankly. The incident took no more than thirty seconds from start to end.

"Fuck that guy," Baldessaro added. "He got off lucky."

Flannery followed Mickey into the damp night air.

"Where's your car?"

The Impala was double-parked in front of the tavern. Rudy's red neon sign reflected on its hood.

"Go on. That mook ain't coming back."

"I don't even know what happened," Mickey managed.

"Don't worry about it. We got you. He knows it too." Flannery nodded toward the Impala. "Go on."

Hands shaking, Mickey dug the keys out of his pocket and drove back to Impact.

Debbie came up to him after class. She wore an oversized thick yellow slicker to ward off the September rain.

"Stalagmites go up from the ground, stalactites down from the ceiling. A mnemonic. G for ground, C for ceiling...And you don't know what I'm talking about."

"No, no, I'm sorry. I'm just not...I'm not here."

"What's wrong?"

Mickey couldn't shake the explosion of violence he witnessed last night. Baldessaro could've killed that man with that bottle-blow across his face.

"I don't know. Geology seems dumber than usual today."

They walked together to the locker-lined hall. Mickey had Macroeconomic Principles in fifteen minutes, which was enough time to load up on cafeteria coffee.

28

A tortoiseshell barrette held back Debbie's auburn hair, revealing sapphire earrings that matched the string around her wrist. "You need to get away," she observed. "My friends and I, we take a place for the summer in Belmar. We're going down to clean it up, steal one last weekend on the beach. Want to join us?"

"When are you leaving?" he asked.

"Friday after class."

"I can't. I work nights."

She said, "Come down on Saturday then. No pressure. We're just hanging."

He hesitated.

"Forget it," she said with a wave. "I hardly know you."

"No, no. I—It sounds great. Can I—Can we do something else? Around here maybe?"

"Sure. Whatever. We can talk rock formations. Limestone."

"Please," Mickey said. "I'm an oaf. Give me a second chance and I'll tell you all about it."

Debbie brightened. "Deal," she said. "See you next week."

"Next week," Mickey agreed.

Mickey sought out Peck and found him walking toward the parking lot, his time card punched.

"Buddy," he shouted, trotting.

Peck stopped. He had his lunch pail at his fist.

They were on a side street in the skyway's shade. "How's your father?"

"Not too good. They put him in a coma."

Mickey expressed his concern.

Peck nodded. Then he said, "I heard what happened. You and that guy."

"Joey saved my ass." Mickey held up his hands, his thin wrists. "Fighting and me...We're strangers."

"You come by Rudy's. I owe you."

29

"I'll say a prayer for your dad," Mickey told him.

Mickey was mid-stride toward Impact when a silver Cadillac pulled to the curb, cutting off his path. Behind the wheel, the driver, in his mid 30s, wore a gray suit, a black turtleneck and an onyx ring. He slid down his sunglasses and looked over the frame.

"You're Wright," the man said.

Concerned, Mickey stepped back. He might have to call for help.

"Joe DeSalvo told me about you. You do the lunch thing, right? Collect the money from everybody."

"Benny Luna collects," Mickey answered cautiously.

He jutted out his left arm. In his hand was a manila envelope. "I'll be by on Friday."

Inside the envelope were strips of paper, long and white, dotted with the names of NFL teams and the betting spread. Lions +7 vs. Packers, Jets +3½ vs. the Patriots and so on.

"Billy Fischetti," the man said. "Billy Fix. Ask around."

He drove off.

During the lunch break, Mickey went to see Luna.

"Do I have to?"

Luna was chewing a sandwich he brought from home. "What do you want me to say, Mick?"

Mickey understood. He had learned Joe DeSalvo was Luna's brother-in-law and godfather to Luna's son, who they called Little Moon, the youngest worker on the dock.

"When you give out the lunch, include a sheet. The other guys, they'll come to you."

Resigned, Mickey headed back toward the office, passing tall cardboard crates awaiting reassignment. Jano approached, a can of Budweiser in hand.

"Are you gonna bet?"

Mickey shook his head. "I mean, *Billy Fix*, for Christ's sake."

"Don't bet once November starts," Jano said. "By then, the

bookies got the spread down tight. Or they know who to pay off. If you have to, go with the dog at home."

Having no idea what Jano was saying, Mickey returned to his desk. Rather than putting the bills of lading in the wire out-box, Broadhead had laid them on Mickey's chair. Point made, Mickey apologized.

"While you're in here, prioritize," Broadhead said without looking up.

By now, Mickey knew retrieving lunch, lying to wives, pulling guys out of bars and running the football pool was the priority, the routing and typing a sideline.

Padding for the shower, Mickey found his father at the kitchen table in his white T, boxers and black socks. Since he started at Impact, Mickey rarely saw him unless Wright was asleep on the couch when he came in, uniform pants undone, shoes kicked aside. Mike Wright made his own hours now. His son was his maid, more or less, dropping the laundry off, filling up the refrigerator. Since Dotty died, Wright was as likely to throw out a dish as wash it. He wrote the checks for the phone bill, the gas and electric, the rent, but left them for Mickey to put in their envelopes and mail. Dust mites the size of raccoons gathered under his rumpled bed.

About the household, they communicated only by inference or a note that required translation: "Elbows. Boil," Wright scrawled. Mickey made a facsimile of his mother's macaroni salad—glob of mayo, canned baby shrimp, celery—and left it in the fridge. Having eaten the entire pound, Wright left the empty Tupperware bowl on the table, serving spoon too. Not a word of thanks nor an offer to share a meal. Not that Mickey minded. The less contact the better, even when they weren't bickering.

"I heard you're doing good at Impact," Wright said now.

Mickey stopped, his outstretched hand halfway to the bathroom door.

"It's a fuckin' miracle."

"Why is it a miracle, Dad?"

"What are you pulling down? Three bills?"

More with overtime. "About. Taxes, Social Security, union dues..."

"Three bills, and he bitches."

"Not bitching. You asked, I answered."

"Joe DeSalvo said you're doing good. He's looking out for you."

What the hell, thought Mickey, *standing there in his ratty old robe with its string belt.* "Who's Billy Fischetti?"

"You met Fischetti?" Wright turned, crossed one pale knee over the other.

"DeSalvo didn't tell you? They have me running the football racket."

"'Racket.'"

"With the slips. The point spreads."

Wright asked, "And what's your take?"

"There's no take. I don't gamble."

"I bet Billy Fix loves that. No take. Jesus. Idiot."

Mickey opened the door. "Yeah, well, nice talking to you, Dad."

"Don't fuck this up," Wright said. "They ask, you do. You don't see it, but you're sitting pretty. DeSalvo's got your back."

Mickey turned on the shower. The water groaned as it made its way up the pipe.

CHAPTER FOUR

A couple of weeks passed without serious incident. Caffaratti hit the football pool twice, winning $200 on two $25 bets. Curiously, he picked the same four teams on consecutive weekends. Little Moon said Caffy didn't know a football from an eggplant, but he was the only winner. Billy Fix was pleased with the crew's ineptitude.

One afternoon, as Mrs. Ada was leaving and Mickey was settling in, Benny Luna came to the office and knocked on the door frame. He looked at Broadhead while pointing at Mickey, who was pulling the carbons and the goldenrod copy from the last manifest Mrs. Ada had typed. Ms. Ada, who spelled "Canaad" thusly.

Mickey joined Luna in the hall.

"Buddy Peck's father died," Luna told him. "Take up a collection after lunch, OK?"

"Sure," Mickey said. Finally, a worthy chore.

"They're burying him out of St. Stephen's in Kearny. Get a Mass card. Maybe go tell Miglio and see if he wants Impact should send a wreath."

"All right."

"Me and my son, we'll go to the wake tomorrow afternoon. You're coming, right?"

Mickey had his American Lit class in the afternoon, but he could blow it off.

At the funeral home, Buddy looked stunned. He tried to gather himself for Benny, but he failed. He looked at Mickey through pitiful eyes.

As Luna and Little Moon knelt at the open casket, Peck said, "You didn't need to come, Mick. But thanks."

"I'm sorry, Buddy," he replied as they shook hands.

"My Dad," he said, shaking his head. "He was my rock. A tougher guy, Mick, you ain't never seen. Now he's..." Peck looked back at the casket. "Ah, you know what I mean."

Mickey nodded, thinking not of his father but of his mother. It didn't seem so long ago he stood before her casket, closed to conceal her emaciated body.

"Come meet my wife and kids," Peck said, taking Mickey by the elbow.

Passing a circle of elderly men, all walkers and canes, they approached a small, somber woman in black, impatient but well-mannered children on either side of her, sheer veil on her head.

How many times have I lied to you, Cheryl Peck? Mickey thought as he took her tiny hand.

Mickey sidled up next to Debbie at the cashier in the St. Peter's cafeteria, their trays bearing an identical lunch of an off-the-grill bacon cheeseburger and shoestring fries. His held, incongruously, a can of Tab.

"Dieting?" she asked.

"I think I'm the guy who likes the taste."

"Not me," Debbie replied. "I use it like an antibiotic. It gets in there and kills all the bad stuff."

They had already met twice for coffee, exchanging vague biographies and shared interests. She had attended Holy Family in Bayonne, where she lived with her family, and was an English major, her ambition to teach high school. Her summer job as a waitress in Belmar gave her the luxury of free time during the school year, her parents supportive. She knew Impact only from seeing the trucks on the turnpike.

"Are you planning on sitting alone again?" she asked now.

"'Again'?"

"I see you sitting here now and then, deep thinking, spooky blue eyes, an orb around you. You should hang a 'Do Not Disturb' sign."

"I invite you to disturb me."

"Hmmm. I don't know what that means, but OK."

As they gathered their trays after the meal, Debbie said, "Let's go out."

"Dinner and a movie?"

"A real date." She bumped his hip. "I'm already excited."

They saw "American Graffiti" in Journal Square, then went to Jersey City's Village section for spaghetti and meatballs. Though they were both under New Jersey's legal drinking age, they shared Chianti poured from a bottle wrapped in wicker.

"Just like 'Lady and the Tramp,'" Debbie said.

I'm smitten, thought Mickey, a novice to dating. He was wearing a new blazer over navy corduroy bell bottoms and Hush Puppies.

When they parked in a shadowy lane near Roosevelt Stadium, Debbie dug a packet of Clorets out of her purse.

"I like garlic as much as the next girl, but…" she said, passing a mint to Mickey.

A week later, they took the PATH train to Greenwich Village and did nothing but walk and gawk, holding hands as they watched an impromptu jam session in Washington Square Park, savoring summer's last gasp. When a girl in tie-dye, a long, flowing skirt and sandals ripped off her top, Debbie said, "Oh, I don't think I'll be doing that."

Mickey averted his eyes, staring instead past the fountain to the arch.

"You're a good boy, Mickey Wright," Debbie said, touching his thigh.

* * *

Jano nominated Mickey as the bank for the World Series pool. The Mets were playing the heavily favored Oakland A's. With a St. Peter's notebook, Mickey walked the dock and collected before the series began. Billy Fix was waiting in the lot when Mickey left to pick up lunch.

Mickey handed over the cash, wrapped around a page torn from the notebook and containing a tally of the bets.

"Heavy on the Mets, right?" Billy Fix said, putting the cash in his jacket pocket.

Mickey nodded.

"The As won twelve more games during the season."

"They like the home team, I guess," Mickey said with a shrug.

A week later, Fix called the office. On his way to Chicken Delight, Mickey met him in the parking lot.

"We're going to take a hit if the Mets win this thing," Fix explained from behind the wheel of his silver Caddy.

Looking through the open passenger-side window, Mickey didn't reply. He knew the Mets had won three games to Oakland's two, but he really didn't follow the sport.

"Maybe you go around again. Talk up the A's. Remind them Oakland's home. Holtzman and Hunter threw good in games one and three. They both won twenty during the season."

Mickey said, "You want them to bet more on the A's now than they bet on the Mets last week."

Fix nodded.

"But they bet with their hearts, no? Would logic persuade them? You give them a second chance and maybe they increase their bets on the Mets."

Twisting his ring, Fix paused in thought. He said, "Yeah, maybe you're right, kid. Fuck it. We'll play the hand they dealt us."

The series ended with the A's winning Game Seven. Billy Fix

returned, handing Mickey a wad of cash that was smaller than what had gone the other way two weeks earlier. "Pay it out," he told him. "Be discreet. Don't fuckin' rub it in." Then he slipped Mickey $50 in crisp tens. "That's yours. Don't tell your old man."

Mickey paid off six winners among the dock crew and the Jersey City-based drivers. Seventeen men lost their bets; Tommy Malzone dropped a week's pay.

"Fuckin' Wayne Garrett," complained Freddy Flannery when he came into the office to use the hand-crank adding machine. "He's the tying run at the plate and he pops up. Two bills down the fuckin' drain."

Jano had a different view. "You think it's on the level?" he asked Mickey. "Why do they let the series go to seven games?"

Before Mickey could reply, Jano said, "To fatten the till. Come on, kid. You really think Willie Mays can't catch two fly balls? Shit…"

Mickey put the five $10 bills in the poor box at Queen of Martyrs. Dirty money he didn't need. He was banking at least $150 a week, even after keeping house for his father and sprucing up his wardrobe for his dates with Debbie. His savings account was swelling and gaining interest at seven percent. The nest egg was real.

Said Billy Fix when he returned with the week's football slips. "Why not run the game yourself? You know by now we don't lay out much. Stash the cash in the safe. If somebody hits, pay him."

"That's not for me," Mickey said directly. "Thanks, though."

"Why not? I heard you're going to be an accountant." Billy Fix laughed. "Might as well get used to handling somebody else's scratch."

"An accountant. Not a bookie."

"What's the difference? You're getting paid for moving money around."

* * *

Mickey heard the sirens overhead, and he thought he smelled smoke. To his surprise, Broadhead wriggled out from behind his desk and went out to the dock. Mickey saw him look up to the skyway, hand on his brow.

"Fire," he said when he returned.

Luna came to the office.

"Mickey, call the cops. Find out what they know. The skyway's closed, the turnpike is backed up to Newark."

While Luna and Broadhead watched, Mickey made the call, first to Jersey City Police Department dispatcher. He knew the number, having used it to page his father when his mother was dying.

A minute or so later, he passed a message onto Luna. "They have no idea when it will reopen."

"Long night," said Luna. "Who's telling Miglio?"

Broadhead pointed to the dock boss.

Mickey looked at the clock. It was coming up on six. Many of the drivers who would have been in already were sitting in traffic. It would be hours before they arrived. Miglio would have to approve overtime for the crew if he wanted to turn around the freight despite the setback. Bedded down at a motel on Tonnelle Avenue, the Canadian drivers were waiting to head north.

Or Miglio might choose to keep a skeleton crew on hand to log in the freight when it arrived and start fresh with all hands tomorrow, maybe bring in the dock crew early.

"I'll call him," Mickey said. "What the hell."

He was in the mood for a fresh adventure, something actually related to what a clerk might do.

Luna had Miglio's home number in his wallet.

Mickey dialed. When one of Miglio's boys answered, Mickey identified himself: "Mchael Wright, I work in the office at Impact."

Miglio came to the phone with a grunt. Mickey imagined the burly man, thick neck, ever in short sleeves, his tie dangling, had stomped to the phone, annoyed at the disturbance, much as he stomped around the day office, perpetually in a sour mood.

Mickey explained.

"Fuck," said Miglio.

"I'm with Benny Luna, Mr. Miglio," Mickey continued. "As far as I can tell, we have three in. Nine are still out. None of the outbound trailers are ready."

Luna had his cap in his hands. He nodded in agreement.

Miglio asked, "How many containers are due?"

When Mickey repeated the question, Luna said, "Three."

"Three," said Mickey.

Some of the containers didn't need to be unloaded. After they were backed to the door, the crew unhitched the local tractor. Luna popped the seal and checked the goods against the manifest, sending Bippo or Little Moon crawling atop the stacked crates and boxes. If all appeared as it should be, the Canada-bound drivers hooked their trailers to the containers and took off, the manifests Mickey typed in their folios and ready for Customs.

"Give me Luna," Miglio said.

Mickey passed over the handset. He watched as Luna nodded, said "yeah," said "OK" and then hung up.

He looked at Mickey. "Yeah, late night. We stay until the containers move out. Anything that comes in before, we handle as usual. After, it sits 'til tomorrow."

"What's the latest you've stayed?" Mickey had Forensic Accounting at 8 a.m.

"Three or four."

"Whoa," said Mickey.

Broadhead cleared his throat. "I leave at midnight," he said.

Luna said, "Show Mickey how to bill."

"I certainly won't be doing that," Broadhead said, puffing up.

Luna shook his head in mild disgust as he departed.

The smell of burning rubber and fuel wafted down from the skyway. Out on the dock, Luna was circled by the crew. He explained what the next few hours might bring.

"I leave at midnight," Broadhead repeated

"All right..." Mickey replied. Returning to his routing book, he said, "What do we do after you go? Seriously."

"Not my concern," Broadhead replied.

"Do we want to face Mr. Miglio if he paid a couple dozen guys hours of overtime and the freight shipped without the charges?"

Broadhead huffed. But he stayed until 2:30 a.m. After typing the last manifest and sweeping up the office, Mickey left an hour later, walking to the lot with Luna, Little Moon, Jano and whoever else stayed for max OT. No one said anything, but Mickey felt fine, especially when Jano gave him a punch on the shoulder, a sign of kinship and approval.

What the hell, he thought. He drove to Corso's to say hello, talk up how they had to scramble at Impact due to the big fire.

Anthony said, "You here to work or bullshit?"

"Bullshit, if you don't mind, Ant," said Mickey.

Too laughed. "Oooh, Wright throws down. You take that lip, Cuz?"

"No, actually I've got an early class," Mickey added. "But I'll Windex."

"Yeah," muttered Anthony, "go Windex."

Sammy handed his son a paper hat as Too washed up.

Freshly shaved but barely awake, Mickey drove to St. Peter's and parked down by Holy Name Cemetery. Halfway up the hill to the campus, he knew he was too fatigued for Forensic Accounting. Instead, he napped on a saggy sofa tucked in a corner of a library corridor. When he woke up, he had no idea where he was. Spinning, sitting up, he kicked over a pile of his books. To his surprise, he discovered he had taken off his carbon-stained sneakers to sleep. He had been out for almost three hours, missing his Macroeconomic Principles class too.

In the Men's Room, he scrubbed his face until he came to his senses. When he looked in the mirror, he saw his hair was in disarray—flat on one side, shooting stalks on the other. He put his head under the faucet, then remembered his brush was in the glove compartment of his Impala. He used a paper towel to make himself close to presentable. There was time for lunch before his Uniform Commercial Code class.

The cold wind prickled his cheeks as he crossed the quad. In the crowded cafeteria, he placed his books on a tray, put two Granny Smith apples and a Yoo-Hoo next to them. Settled, he took a long swig of the chocolate drink, then fished out the thick UCC class text. He found the subject baffling—more history of how the code came to be than how it could be practically applied. Mickey thought of his studies at St. Peter's as vocational, despite the Geology and American Lit electives, so he had figured UCC would teach him something about leases and banking in broad strokes. Now reading a baffling passage that required a second and third glance, Mickey bit the cap off his yellow marker to highlight it, as if that would make it register.

"Nice hair."

Cap between his teeth, he looked up to see Debbie on the other side of the table. Without realizing he had, he brought his hand to the side of his head.

She opened her leather tote bag and passed over a brush. "Want me to do it?" she asked.

"Would you?"

"Here? No."

Debbie wore a brown knee-length coat over a violet turtleneck and jeans. Her hair was tucked under a stocking cap. He stared up into her moon face and midnight eyes, and all of a sudden, he forgot about the Uniform Commercial Code.

He returned the brush as she sat.

"You're dressed for the weather."

"I hate the cold. Brrr," she said, eyeing his apples. "Health kick?"

"The corned beef back there looks like it's been around since St. Patrick's Day," he said as he gave her a Granny Smith.

Polishing it dramatically on her sleeve, Debbie said, "I'm reluctant to ask since you so rudely rejected me the first time—"

"When did I reject you? I could never."

"Belmar. End of the summer."

"You still think about that?"

"Never mind." She chomped into the apple. "Oh, that's juicy. What are you doing on Saturday?"

Sleeping, thought Mickey. Vacuuming. Food shopping. "Seeing you?"

"My parents are going away for the weekend. You want to come over?"

"Define 'come over.'"

"Spend the night," she said.

"Really?"

"And all it entails. I'm nervous. Say yes."

"Yes."

"Oh thank God," Debbie sighed.

Mickey smiled. "Hey Deb, are you my girlfriend?"

Another chomping bite. "I'm not seeing anybody else. You?"

He shook his head.

"Ask."

"Deb, will you be my girlfriend?"

"Already am, Mickey. Make a plan for the whole day, OK. Call me tonight."

As she came around the table, she put her hand on his shoulder and, as if whispering to him, leaned in and kissed his ear.

CHAPTER FIVE

They went to the Metropolitan Museum of Art to see an exhibition of photography by Ansel Adams, Debbie telling Mickey how her father clipped Adams' photos out of *Life* and *National Geographic* and tacked them to a corkboard in his home office. He was a sales manager with the Squibb Corporation, his territory north to Hartford. Mickey had met Debbie's mom; she worked part time at the phone company. The Olsens had a brick house with a porch on a quiet block across from a leafy park and a few softball fields. If anything in southern Hudson County could be called bucolic, it was Debbie's neighborhood, which was a short walk from Newark Bay and far from the city's shipyards and refineries.

The museum was crowded on a chilly Saturday. After Adams, they slalomed their way past strollers, walkers and gaggles of tourists whispering in native languages to find the Japanese collection. Debbie was intrigued, Mickey intimidated. She knew something; he knew nothing. He thought to confess he had never been in a museum outside of school field trips, but he kept it to himself. Debbie spent five minutes cooing over a foot-high 11th century Buddhist deity.

As they began walking down Fifth Avenue, Debbie told Mickey her brother Warren Jr. had been killed in Vietnam; she said her parents shielded her from their suffering, but she missed him terribly. She was a kid when he left, she said. It would've been nice to know him now when he could see her as a peer.

"He thought I was a pain. Mostly, he told me to get lost."

"You were like that, huh?"

"I can be powerfully annoying, Mickey," she replied. "You'd be surprised."

They walked on for a while along Fifth Avenue, Central Park holding on to its last leaves, gray cobblestone under foot, and they passed the French Consulate and the Frick Collection, the air growing colder as the sun moved further west. If he wasn't so contented, Mickey would've thought it was too much, too corny, straight out of Archie comics—Debbie holding his hand, smiling; her Frye boots; her bell bottoms, a navy cabled sweater.

"Do you have any brothers or sisters?" Debbie asked. They waited to cross at 65th Street, the children's zoo beyond the brownstone wall.

"I do. Rosemary. She's five years older than me."

"And?"

Jack hesitated. "I don't know where she is. She and my father, they don't get along."

"You don't hear from her?"

He shook his head. "She was pregnant when she left. He doesn't know I know. I could find her, I guess. She went to St. Dominic's. I could ask around."

"So, you have a niece or a nephew somewhere. Maybe she named him after you."

Mickey laughed. "I doubt it. I'm a junior. She would name him X before she called him Michael."

Dull-eyed and hunched, white horses were in a queue, breath steaming out their nostrils, their carriages awaiting hardy tourists. Yellow taxis idled alongside the Plaza Hotel. "The Way We Were" was playing at the Paris Theater.

"You don't like your father, do you?"

"I wouldn't say it like that," Mickey replied. "But two men, small apartment. To tell you the truth, I was my mom's son."

"Cancer," she recalled.

"I miss her. She would've liked you, Deb. You would've made her smile."

They went on in silence again. Traffic was slowed by construction up ahead, and an appliance-store delivery truck seemed to follow them as it crept along the avenue. Mickey suggested they stop at Rockefeller Center to watch the ice skaters. Debbie was amendable despite the wind. She told Mickey she was having the best day.

They made love on her single bed, tenderly, in rhythm, gentle moans, bodies glistening. Afterwards, Debbie went "oh my, my, my," and giggled and Mickey lay with his head on her stomach; he twirled her dark pubic hair. They kissed again, they held each other; she ran a finger along his spine. When he shivered, they laughed.

Debbie put on Mickey's shirt and left the bedroom. He studied her room—her desk, paperbacks in disarray in a bookcase, framed photos taken down the shore, her friends on the beach; a framed photo of her brother in his high-school football uniform. An accordion near her closet door. Twilight through the thin curtains. Most of those albums were her brothers', she'd said; Warren Junior preferred the Stones to the Beatles. She did not. "John or Paul?" she asked Mickey who, having given it no prior thought, said, "Ringo." Motown was her favorite. "I like Motown," said Mickey. "Martha Vandella, right?" He heard Rosemary singing "Nowhere to Run," saw her hop-skip dancing to "American Bandstand."

Debbie returned with two tall glasses of iced tea. She hung his shirt on the back of her desk chair. Naked again, she said, "Music? Your call."

He deferred.

She chose Marvin Gaye's "What's Going On."

He heard men's chattering voices, then a soaring saxophone—

45

Mickey saw a bird floating, drifting in an open sky—and then Gaye entered, his voice sweet yet purposeful.

"Dance with me, Mickey," said Debbie, who swayed to the music.

He left the bed, and they embraced, rocking gently. Now Mickey heard strings, hand drums, a distant xylophone. He took in Debbie's scent. The braided throw rug tickled his feet.

She said, "I know this is heavy stuff. Social commentary. But this song is freedom to me. I remember...We were driving on the boulevard, a bunch of us girls from Holy Family, and it was a sunny day in spring and I felt so free. I don't know...It was like I realized my childhood had ended and I was about to begin the next thing. This song, it takes me right back there. You know?"

He said, "I'm thinking whenever I hear it, I'm going to remember this moment. This one, right here, right now. Forever."

They kissed.

Debbie reached to the turntable, lifted the arm, flipped over the album, and dropped the needle on a new upbeat song. She spun as she danced away from him. Mickey watched her, his eyes running up and down her body.

"Come on, Mickey," she said. "Dance with me."

"I can't dance."

"You can dance."

"I am telling you, no, I can't."

He retreated to the bed, jumped in, pulled up the sheet.

He thought, I think I'm falling in love with this woman, this free woman, that smile, those eyes, that body, little belly, wide hips, her arms in the air. Look how she shines.

"What?" she said as she twirled.

"I'm happy."

"Me too."

He inched aside and tapped the mattress.

Turning down the volume, she joined him, nestling in his arms.

* * *

Debbie woke to an empty bed. Mickey was over there at her desk, dressed, but his shirt was unbuttoned, one beige Hush Puppie untied. Wiping the sleep from her eyes, she saw he had taken "The Great Gatsby" from her shelf and was quietly reading.

"Sneaking out?" she said, after clearing her throat.

"I didn't want to wake you."

The nightstand clock read 5:50. Beyond her window, the sky was a deep blue and the streets were silent.

"Gatsby."

"There's bound to be an essay on the exam," he replied.

She sat up and tugged the sheet to cover her breasts. "Don't go on about the green light on the Daisy's dock or the eyes of T.J. Eckleburg, the optometrist."

"We spent a half-a-semester in high school on the symbolism—"

"Well, that's high school, isn't it? Stick to Chapter Nine— Nick's musings after the funeral. It's all there. Or how Daisy is vapid and unworthy of worship. She never pays, does she? She gets away with killing Myrtle. And Gatsby too, if you think about it."

Mickey held the paperback as if offering it to her.

"Don't need it." She tapped the side of her head. "But come back to bed, Mickey. It's cozy…"

"I can't," he said, bending to tie his shoe. "Mass."

"The Latin one. Can I come?"

"Sure," he said.

"Can we have that bread you go on about afterwards?"

"Absolutely." If he was going to introduce her to anyone in his life, it might as well be the Corsos.

She popped out of bed. "Give me 10 minutes." She scooted out of the bedroom. Then she returned immediately.

"This is a real romance, isn't it? I'm giddy."

She disappeared before he could respond.

* * *

One frigid November night, as he swept the carbon paper from the office floor, Mickey heard gunfire. Setting aside the push broom, he put on his parka and crept warily toward the dock. At the far end, well beyond Benny Luna's booth, a crowd gathered, mostly the younger crew members, second-generation Teamsters. As he drew nearer, Mickey saw Little Moon firing rounds from a cannon-sized pistol toward beer cans on a rail over by the repair shop.

Flames danced as broken pallets burned in oil barrels. Between sips of cold brew, the crowd cheered him on. Little Moon closed an eye and took a shot. Groans and laughter as the bullet missed its target.

Little Moon looked at the gun as if it were to blame. Then he turned to Caffy. "What the fuck are you laughing at?" he said, glowering.

Caffy grew stiff. He began to shuffle. "No. I just…"

"Shut it, fuckface. Now."

Caffy retreated.

Blowing into his fist, Little Moon set up again, feet apart, arm outstretched, and squeezed the trigger. The can flew into the air. He let out of a whoop as the crew applauded and clapped his back.

He spotted Mickey at the edge of the crowd. "You want a shot, College?" he asked.

The crowd parted.

"Go ahead, College Boy," Mo Brennan said, nudging Mickey.

Sheepish, Mickey declined.

"No, no, that's a good idea," Little Moon said. "You don't know what you're doing, and the recoil takes off the side of your fuckin' head."

"What is it?" Mickey asked. "It's huge."

"It's a .44 Magnum. Smith & Wesson Model 29. Six-and-a-half inch barrel."

48

He handed it to Mickey, who hefted it. "It's a load," he said, giving it back.

"You seen 'Dirty Harry'? This is Dirty Harry's gun, man. Bullet cuts through a fuckin' engine block. It'd slice a mother-fucker in half."

Brennan asked for a chance to shoot it, allowing Mickey to retreat and return to his broom. When he clocked out at 12:45 a.m., Little Moon was still shooting at beer cans, the crowd still cheering him on.

When Mickey returned the next day, the crew lingered in the parking lot, the cry of the horn several minutes away. Curious, he walked deep into the mechanics' bay, where he found a wall chipped and pock-marked, the result of Little Moon's .44. Spent bullets were scattered on the oily blacktop.

Later, Benny Luna came by the office, asked Mickey step outside. Broadhead looked up but silently deferred to the dock boss.

Said Luna, "Forget what you seen."

"The gun?"

"Don't tell nobody," he added.

"Of course."

By now, Mickey was the bearer of many secrets, the teller of many lies. Eddie Grossi broke his leg racing around on a forklift after hours; Jano told Mickey, who heard the crash, no, you tell Miglio and the insurance guys he fell when the forklift jammed. Earlier in the same week, he had heard angry shouting on the dock. Leaving his typewriter, he went outside to witness two men about Benny Luna's age arguing, O'Brien manning a dolly, Zielinski near pallets of leather goods bound for Sainte-Anne-de-Sabrevois, Quebec. As profanities flew, the men's sons joined in and almost immediately began swinging at each other. Mickey retreated. Every fight he had ever witnessed ended quickly with grabbing and clutching. But they exchanged thunderous punches to each other's face and head. Blood flowed. No one spoke, no one intervened. Finally, the two young men spilled into the Strick and one of the men tumbled over a crate, landing heavy on the bay. Now the other dock workers jumped in, restraining one man, helping up the other. Luna was at the edge of the crowd. "Back to work," he said calmly. He looked at the older men, the fathers, with disapproval bordering on disgust.

Mickey approached him. In the office was a first-aid kit. He asked Luna if he should bring it out.

"To do what?" said Luna. "Nothing happened. You didn't see nothing."

Even his father was telling him to ignore trouble. Coming back from Sam Chin's with shirts on hangers and a duffel bag bursting with clean clothes, Mickey ran into him as he entered their apartment building. In uniform, Wright pulled the door shut; the two men stood in the little vestibule, mailboxes and buzzers at Mickey's back.

"Who's this Bippo?" Wright asked.

Mickey dropped the duffel. He hung the shirts on the door-knob. "He works on the dock."

"You know him?"

Mickey was looking at the ridges the hangers had dug into his hand. "Not really."

"The whores in the parking lot...The mattress in the Stricks."

Mickey looked at his father, his expression revealing his surprise.

"You don't know?"

He shook his head.

"I'm not asking if they threw you a blow job—"

"Dad. Jesus."

"Stay away," Wright warned. "It's not sanctioned. DeSalvo is coming down on him. If he don't stop, it'll be me."

Mickey picked up the sack

"Don't say nothing to nobody."

"I won't."

* * *

50

His father ran into him a week later. They hadn't seen each other since the brief conversation in the vestibule, at least not while both were awake. A couple of days ago, Wright had left his son half an egg salad on rye and a soggy pickle on a paper sack on the kitchen table. "I don't want it," Wright wrote, failing to anticipate how the mayo would curdle in the steam heat.

On campus now and with a few minutes to spare, Mickey grabbed a Hostess Sno Ball out of a vending machine and unwrapped it as he made his way across the quad, its red brick pathways slick from a drizzling rain, the spindly trees barren. When he heard his name, he had chocolate filling in his teeth, pink frosting on his lips.

In uniform, Wright walked toward him.

Mickey put the Sno Ball in his parka pocket. "What's wrong?"

"I saw Joe DeSalvo."

Passing students looked at them, a college kid and a cop. St. Peter's tended to lean conservative under the Jesuits, but who around here trusted cops after the race riots in Newark and Plainfield, Hurricane Carter in Paterson and then the televised beatings of protesters in Chicago back in '68?

"DeSalvo? The Teamsters? Remember?" Wright said.

"Yeah, I know," Mickey said.

"Let's go sit in the car. I'm getting wet out here."

"Dad, I got class in like 10 minutes."

"Mickey, you're not listening. Joe DeSalvo. Be late for the goddamned class."

They walked toward the squad car. Double-parked on a two-way side street that ran along the campus, its engine was running, and oily clouds billowed from its rattling tailpipe. Mike Wright pointed to the passenger's side door. As his son settled in, he walked around the car, staring toward the traffic backed up to the boulevard.

Seated behind the wheel, Wright dug into his coat pocket. He pulled out a booklet of raffle tickets.

"These are from DeSalvo," he said as he passed the booklet to his son.

Mickey read the top sheet. The Jersey City Democratic Society was raffling off a trip for two to Bermuda.

"Fifty dollars a pop. You do Impact."

Mickey was still reading the coupon. Second prize was a night for two at the Hilton by Newark Airport. Dinner and Champagne.

"Not just the crew, but the day office. Everybody kicks in. They say Vince Miglio likes you, so don't be shy."

"Fifty dollars is a lot of money." He looked at his father. "Do they do it every year?"

"Every year. But don't let this slide. The idea is to get them before they start shopping for Christmas. Make them think if they drop fifty dollars, they'll be putting Bermuda under the tree."

"I'm no salesman, Dad."

"And you take one too. Maybe you take two and show Eddie Swayback you're grateful."

"So this is the Teamsters fronting for the Democrats?"

"'Fronting'?" Wright laughed. "That's what you're learning at Impact? Yeah, 'fronting.'"

Mickey was feeling the task was better suited to Billy Fix. "What if someone says no?"

Mike Wright said, "You tell Luna or you tell me. But nobody is saying no."

Mickey flipped through the booklet. There were two hundred tickets numbered 2800 to 3000. He was responsible for collecting $10,000. "Who holds the take?"

"Bring it home. Now get moving. I've got to run."

Mickey put the booklet in his pocket.

"And clean off your face, for Christ's sake." He shook his head. "Cupcake. Still like a fuckin' child."

CHAPTER SIX

Mickey opened the pneumatic tube and frowned when he looked at the destination on the bill of lading. Throwing on the hoodie he kept on the coat tree, he went out to see Luna.

"Benny," he said, knocking on the shack.

Luna looked over his bifocals. He gestured for Mickey to step inside.

He had a space heater near his feet. Its coils glowed red and hot.

"Look at this. It's going to Ottawa, Illinois, not Ottawa, Ontario."

Luna studied the paperwork. A pallet of burner grates was supposed to go to Illinois.

"Send it through Mississauga. Let the Canadians worry about it."

"If I do, I'll look like an idiot."

"Mickey," Benny teased in sing-song, "who's going to think you're an idiot? You, our College Boy."

As he returned toward the office, the lunchtime run an hour off, Mickey felt a tug on his sleeve. Bippo pulled him into a half-emptied box truck.

"I know it was you," Bippo said angrily. He wore an Army field parka, a stocking cap and his work gloves.

Mickey snapped his arm free. "It was me what?"

"You ratted us out."

The whores. "Wasn't me. I didn't know a thing about it."

Bippo narrowed his beady eyes and jabbed him with a finger. "You told your old man."

"My old man told me, Bip. Knowing you, you probably couldn't keep your mouth shut."

Mickey turned to walk away.

"You don't fool me," Bippo shouted. "You ain't no saint."

"Fuck off," said Mickey Wright, surprising himself.

Bippo ran after him, cutting him off. "What did you say?"

"I said, 'Fuck off.'"

Bippo fidgeted, shuffling in place. He hadn't expected the response, the Wright kid staring at him. Shifting his eyes, he looked to see who was watching College Boy stand up

"Get the fuck out of here," he said finally.

Mickey waited, then stepped around the Bippo.

"Your old man don't scare me."

"Well, maybe he should, huh?"

"Fuck you."

Backpedaling, Mickey said, "Got it. Fuck me. Fuck my father. Noted."

Back in the office, Mickey hung up his hoodie, routed the bill of lading to Mississauga and, rather than dump it in the basket, walked it over to Broadhead.

Broadhead sighed and took the bill.

"Benny says send it. I tried."

"Ridiculous."

Mickey said, "I can ask upstairs to call the shipper. We can hold the freight until they decide."

"You would like that, wouldn't you? To impress Miglio."

"Oh, for Christ's sake." He took back the bill.

"I won't you speak to me like that," Broadhead said. "You may think you walk on water—"

"I'm just trying to do the job. You know?"

Face red, Broadhead said, "You're not the only one who knows Ed Swayback."

"What the heck does Ed Swayback have to do with Ottawa, Illinois?"

"You're not the only one who knows Ed Swayback."

"I give up," Mickey moaned as he sat, grabbing his forehead. "What's the right thing? Please. Tell me."

Broadhead went back to his paperwork

Mickey pulled a piece of stationery from the desk, wrote "Hold it" in block letter across it, then stapled it to the bill of lading. He raised it up for Broadhead to see.

"OK?"

No reply.

Mickey put the paperwork in the pneumatic tube and sent it out to Luna.

Forty-five minutes later, Mickey was back at Luna's shack to pick up the lunch order. He looked at the sheet. Sandwiches from Monteleone's.

"Broadhead told you to hold it?" Luna said, coming up behind him, clipboard in hand.

"He threw Councilman Swayback in my face. But, yeah, he won't route it."

"You want me to tell Joe about him?"

DeSalvo, Luna's brother-in-law.

Mickey said, "Nah. But he's still pissed we went to Vince with the skyway fire."

"Like he shoulda done. You know he had a crackup before he came here, right? They put him in a home."

"Really? That might explain it. Most nights he's like a robot."

"They probably got him doped up. But, yeah, we'll pull the shipment. Tell the day office."

Mickey nodded.

Luna laughed. "Bippo and Broadhead. Some night for you, huh?"

What the hell, Mickey thought. "Do the guys think I ratted out Bippo and the whores?"

"I know they don't," Luna said, rubbing his cold hands

together. "For one, it was me that called Joe. Whores in the parking lot. Are you kidding me? Two, you call the union to step in, they like that." Luna made a tight fist. "So...Fuck Bippo."

"Thanks, Benny," Mickey said.

Luna nodded slowly, knowingly.

Now Mickey was back with a carton of sandwiches and paper napkins. Luna punched the horn, and the crew gathered.

One by one, Mickey handed out the food. "Jano," he said, then slapped a sandwich into his hand. "Caffy." "Al Zielinski." "O'Brien, Ed. O'Brien, Sean." "Tut-Tut." "Bippo."

Snarling, Bippo snatched his meal.

"I'm you, Bip," said Jano, as he unwrapped his sandwich, "I check to see the kid didn't shit in it."

Bippo eyed Mickey with suspicion. "Fuck it." He ripped open the butcher paper.

Mickey had had no trouble off-loading the raffle chances. Everybody on the dock ponied up: The deal was a combination of gambling and civic responsibility, though a few of the guys paid without enthusiasm as if acknowledge they had no choice but to kick back to the political party the Teamsters were in bed with. Broadhead stood, took out his wallet, handed Mickey five $10 bills and went back to his rate book. Upstairs, Miglio bought 10 tickets. Every local trucker, including Impact's sole black driver, Minnow Duckett, took two. The Canadians wanted in. Soon, Mickey had no more to sell. When Bobo Watson, a part-time mechanic, complained he'd been shut out, Mickey, half-kidding, offered him one of his chances for $100. Bobo said no, adding, "I got no shot, anyway. Luck ain't my friend."

"You got a gift for this," said Mike Wright, standing in the

kitchen in his boxers and undershirt, the morning coffee perco-
lating. He peered at the currency his son had passed to him in
an Impact envelope. "Anybody say no?"

Aileen Murphy, the one-woman Personnel Department,
declined, as did Mrs. Ada. Hennie Adamczyk, a local driver,
passed as well: He had a son with cerebral palsy and explained,
in a way that embarrassed Mickey, that he couldn't swing it.

"No," Mickey told his father. "All in."

The unreliable radiator clanked and hissed.

"Dad, are you working Thanksgiving?"

"Don't worry about me," Wright replied.

"I'm asking."

Last year, they went to the All-Star for turkey with gloppy
gravy, an ice-cream scoop of mashed potatoes, gray-green string
beans, cranberry sauce that still bore the mold of the can. "Just
like your mother used to make," Wright said. Mickey agreed. It
was that bad.

"You're going to your girl's, right?"

Debbie had invited him, yes. "My girl?"

"The new clothes, new shoes. The after shave. I seen how
you clean up. Don't bullshit me."

"Debbie," Mickey said. "She goes to St. Peter's."

"So, you're having Thanksgiving with her. Good. Think I
give a shit?"

"Dad, I think you do not give a shit. But I told her I'd check
with you."

The coffee began to percolate on the stove. Briefly, Mickey
thought of his mother. Firing up the old dented pot was her
morning's first chore. Mickey would listen from under the
covers as she made the coffee, then went off to the bathroom to
clean up, run a bristly brush through her hair. In her housecoat
and bare feet, she would then cross the living room, tug her
son's toe, rattle Rosemary's mattress, and then repeat as she
made the trip back toward the kitchen. By the time Mickey and
his sister reached the table, runny eggs and burnt bacon or

maybe watery oatmeal with brown sugar awaited. Dotty looked at her kids with pride as she sipped her coffee.

"Don't worry about me," Wright said now.

"It's not a matter of worry. I don't want you to be alone on Thanksgiving."

Wright grabbed an old mug from the cabinet. "Because I ain't with you, I'm alone? Dumb."

Mickey waited as his father poured a steaming cup.

"Smells good," Mickey said.

"You think I can't make a cup of coffee. If I want, I can make a fuckin' turkey, too."

"Coffee smells good, Dad," Mickey said as he turned toward the bathroom.

Mickey checked himself again as he walked toward the Olsens'. Hush Puppies brushed, crisp crease in his cords, dress shirt starched and pressed, blazer hanging just right. Despite the snapping wind off Newark Bay, he left his parka in his Impala: Better for a tidy presentation, a well-kempt St. Peter's boy with an eye to detail, a young man of promise. He carried a bouquet in his right hand. He cupped his mouth to check his breath. Ultra Brite fresh.

He walked up the steps and rang the bell. Debbie's father answered. Though he had seen a photo, Mickey was surprised by his appearance: taller than he had imagined, more than thin than fit, a bit hunched, furrowed brow, a cautious smile.

"Mr. Olsen. I'm Mickey Wright."

"Of course. Warren Olsen." They shook hands. "Pleasure to meet you, Mickey."

Mickey stepped into the warm house. Debbie emerged from the kitchen, dish towel in hand, smiling, hurrying toward him. She kissed Mickey's cheek, giving him a little hug.

"Flowers?"

"Happy Thanksgiving," he said. The Olsen home was scented

by roasting turkey.

Mr. Olsen waved his arm. "Come in, Mickey. Warm yourself by the fire."

Debbie said, "I'll put these in water."

Mickey walked toward the flames in the brick fireplace. The leather Barcalounger was Mr. Olsen's preferred seat. An open copy of the *New York Times* lay tented on the cushion and his pipe was in its ashtray on the end table.

In a beige blazer, white shirt and tie, and brown slacks, Mr. Olsen pointed Mickey to the sofa. "Something to drink?"

As he sat, Mickey said, "No, sir, I don't think so."

"Fine."

He turned when Mr. Olsen peered past him toward the kitchen.

Mickey stood. "Hello, Mrs. Olsen."

Round, dark and bright-eyed like her daughter, she wore a frilly apron over gray-green knee-length one-piece dress.

She came toward him and brushed his cheek with hers. "Thank you for the flowers, Mickey. Warren, did you offer our guest a drink?"

"Done and declined."

She said, "We'll be ready in about a half-hour, Mickey."

He nodded.

"Debra?" said Mrs. Olsen, crooking her index finger. "Back to work..."

"You're abandoned," Debbie told Mickey as she followed her mother toward the kitchen.

Back in his seat, Mr. Olsen said, "Debbie's told us a bit about you, Mickey. An Accounting major, I understand. But you're interested in baking?"

Mickey smiled sheepishly. "I have a sort of apprenticeship at a local bakery. It's good work. Satisfying in a way, I don't know, accounting isn't, at least not yet. It's vague at the moment."

Shut up, Mickey, he told himself.

"And you work at Impact Trucking..."

He nodded. "In the office. Router and typist."

"It's a Teamster outfit, isn't it?"

"Yes, sir," said Mickey, who suddenly felt on the defense. "For some reason, the office personnel is in a trucker's union. It doesn't make much sense."

"But the pay is good, I imagine."

Mickey nodded lightly. Then he said, "Debbie told me your territory extends all the way to Hartford."

Warren Olsen smiled, nodded. "Glad I don't cover it myself, though. I manage three sales offices in the tri-state area. Sixty reps."

"Squibb, right? Antibiotics, cancer drugs..."

"You've done your research."

"I lost my Mom to cancer, sir."

"Debbie told us. I'm sorry, Mickey. Awful disease." He reached for his pipe. "Your father is a policeman?"

"And I have a sister. Rosemary. She's a wanderer."

Mr. Olsen packed his tobacco with his thumb. "Something quite appealing about that, isn't there?"

Mickey looked toward the fireplace and the family photos on the mantle including one of Warren Jr. in his fatigues and Debbie in her high school cap-and-gown. He looked at the books in the built-in cabinet, the cushy, cozy furniture and the lace curtains on the windows, everything just so and just right. As Mr. Olsen's question hung in the air, Mickey thought wandering an inadequate substitute for a home of a loving family.

Debbie returned with an iced tea for Mickey and what looked like a Scotch on the rocks for her father.

"Don't think me a reprobate, Mickey."

Mickey laughed.

"He judges up, Dad. Mickey is the world's last optimist."

"Well, he's young..." Mr. Olsen said with a wry smile.

The meal was a delight, the bird moist, the roasted potatoes crispy on the outside, fluffy within. The Olsens served stuffing feathered with chestnuts and sage. Fresh peas. Debbie made the cranberry sauce not by opening a can but by boiling the berries with orange juice and sugar. Laughing easily, the Olsens finished each other's sentences: recalling the tension as they ate the first holiday meal Mrs. Olsen cooked for her stern future mother-in-law who felt dethroned or the time they found Warren Jr., aged three or so, sitting on the kitchen table gnawing on a turkey wing before the meal was served—"While still attached to the carcass, mind you," Mr. Olsen told Mickey—and the ill-fated Thanksgiving in Hilton Head that was interrupted by a hurricane. "A storm, Warren," Mrs. Olsen said, "but yes. A disaster."

"Force majeure," he shrugged. "Advice from on high: Stay home on holidays, Olsens."

Mickey had little to contribute by way of heart-warming Thanksgiving tales. A story of the annual buildup to his father and Rosemary shouting "fuck you" over a desert-dry bird and desiccated lima beans wouldn't play. Nor would the saga of his father's partner Dietz turning up at their apartment with his girlfriend while his wife was sitting on the sofa, chatting with Dotty and Father Stan. God, how Rosemary howled.

"I hope you saved room for dessert, Mickey," Mrs. Olsen said.

"I can be persuaded," he replied.

She suggested he and her husband exit while she and Debbie cleared the dining-room table.

As he stood, Mr. Olsen held up a finger. "I'll show Mickey my inner sanctum."

"Oh God, Dad..."

Mickey folded his napkin.

They went upstairs to Mr. Olsen's office,. His desk was prepared for office work: pen-and-pencil set, Squibb stationery, a legal pad, calendar, Rolodex, phone.

"A telex," Mickey said as he followed Mrs. Olsen inside.

"Rarely used," he replied as he sat at his desk. "This was my son's bedroom. He was a handful. But, yes, I do miss him. Not a day goes by when I don't wonder what would've become of him. I support President Nixon—it's our duty, Mickey. But my son deserved better. Much better."

As Mr. Olsen filled a pipe, Mickey wandered to the long, wide corkboard. As Debbie had indicated, it was coated in magazine clippings of photos: snowcapped mountains beyond rows of pines, lanky trees reflected in an ice-smooth lake, snake-like roots of a tree, the moon suspended above a proud promontory.

"Is this him? Ansel Adams?"

"As a young man, yes. He's in his mid 70s now."

"God. America is a big ol' beautiful place, isn't it? You could just lose yourself in it."

"Mickey," he said, "come here. Take a seat."

Mr. Olsen rolled his chair toward his tall filing cabinet and removed a bottle of port and two cordial glasses.

"Just for us," he said as he filled the glasses.

Mickey eyed the bottle with curiosity.

"No worries, son. You've already had a taste. It was in Sharon's gravy."

He handed a glass to Mickey. As he raised his, he said, "To big ol' beautiful America."

Mickey nodded. Sipping the port, he felt warmth spread across his chest.

Mr. Olsen lit his pipe. A plume of blue smoke rose from the tobacco.

"Mickey, I sense Debbie is very fond of you. No, more so. I sense she loves you. And you love her, I assume."

"I do," he replied nervously. The room seemed small.

"Would you say you're serious?"

"We haven't gotten that far," Mickey said. "But we're true, if that makes sense."

"You're ambitious, Mickey. That's admirable. And you respect my daughter. I can see that."

Mickey sipped the sweet port.

"What are your intentions, if I may ask?"

He hesitated. "My intentions are to finish St. Peter's. From there on, I don't know. One day, it's the Culinary Institute in Hyde Park, the next day it's an MBA."

"You're saving your pay..."

"I do. I am."

Mr. Olsen set aside the pipe. "She's all we have now, Mickey."

He nodded.

"Of course, we're cautious. Overly so. I think I'm right to say she's never been in love before."

"Mr. Olsen—"

"One moment."

He opened the top drawer of his desk, removed a slip of paper and slid it across the blotter.

It was a raffle ticket from the Jersey City Democratic Society.

"You gave this to Debbie, yes?"

Mickey swayed as if the room had moved.

"We can't accept. You need to know, Mickey, this is not us. Forgive me, but Jersey City politics is filthy. The Teamsters, I'm sure you've heard. I don't know your father—"

"My father?"

"Mickey." Mr. Olsen leaned in. "As I said, she's all we have."

"I don't know what you heard about my father—"

"Yes you do, Mickey. Yes you do. But you're a different breed. I see that. This game they play...It's not for you. You have plans."

Mickey sat back. "Why do I have the feeling you're insulting me with compliments?"

"Or complimenting you with insults. Neither. Both. Long/short: Debbie isn't hitching her star to Jersey City thugs who depend on political largesse for their livelihood and will do whatever they must. Not even by a degree of separation."

"And that's my father? A Jersey City thug."

"Not my concern. I only care if it's you. If I had to, right now, I would wager it's not. Church, your studies, your ambitious, the way you carry yourself. Courtesy, inquisitiveness. I see a very fine young man."

"I hope so," he replied, though hardly placated.

"The company you keep, Mickey..." With an index finger, he pushed the raffle ticket until it was atop the base of his pen-and-pencil set.

They had talked about going to Journal Square to catch a movie, but no, Mickey said now. He was tired after a long holiday following a late night at Impact; and now sleep-inducing tryptophan coursed through his bloodstream. Affecting a pout, Debbie moaned with disappointment under an evening sky that promised snow.

"Did you have a good time at least?" she asked. "I can't tell."

"I did. Maybe the best meal ever."

"And...?"

"It was great. They're very generous."

"Mickey..." She stopped, folding her arms across the front of her long cloth coat. "What's wrong?"

"Your father doesn't approve of me. But, you know, so what?"

"Really? 'So what?'"

"Not 'so what,' but—"

"What did he say?"

Headlights of a passing car swept across them. "'Jersey City thug.' My father's a dirty cop."

"He called you a thug?"

"No. He suggested I'm part of a gang of thugs. 'The company I keep.'"

"You must've misunderstood. I could tell he liked you. He

took you seriously. You—No, wait, let me finish. You yourself say you aren't like those guys at Impact. And the Teamsters. It's not a secret, Mickey, what they do."

"I'm not them."

"I'm sure he knows that now. Mickey, listen." She held onto his arms. "I was loving the hell out of you at the table. You *glowed*. I think my mother wants to adopt you."

Another car drove by. "He gave me back the raffle ticket."

"Well, he is a Republican..."

"It wasn't that. He treated it like an insult."

She said, "I'm sure he knew you were being generous."

Mickey shook his head. "No. He knew I had to offload them. Because that's the game they play. He doesn't want you anywhere near that game."

"Can you blame him? Think about it. That's not his world. After the war, he got his degree via the G.I. Bill. He started as a trainee at Squibb. It took him years to break into Sales management. He's not likely to respect men who rely on kickbacks and bribery to get ahead."

"I'm not bribing anybody. It was a gift. Just a gift."

"Is he wrong to be suspicious?" She sighed. "Mickey...If you weren't saving up to move out and go to grad school, would you stay there?"

"At Impact? Probably not."

"Because you know that's not for you. You know it. You know it doesn't, I don't know, *correspond* with who you are."

He hung his head.

"You're your mother's son. And I love you for it."

She nestled into him, putting her arms around his waist. He hesitated, then hugged her tight. They kissed.

"He wanted to know if we're serious," he said.

"I'm seriously cold out here. Start up the car and let's have a little time together."

He dipped into his pocket for his keys.

CHAPTER SEVEN

A vice principal at the county Voc-Tech school won the raffle and the trip to Bermuda. According to *the Jersey Journal*, second prize went to a trucker at an abattoir in Secaucus. He was a native of Puerto Rican, which upset the Impact crew more so than the apparent fix that ensured the top prize for the niece of a state senator.

"Mark my words," said Bippo to the gathering crew as Mickey set down lunch on the cable reel. "The shitbags are taking over."

Walush was pissing off the edge of the dock.

Mickey said nothing. Milling in the sub-freezing temperature, the dock crew was already miffed at him for refusing to accept individual orders for Chicken Delight: "Two wings." "No wings." "All white meat." "I ain't paying extra for white meat." Instead, he bought a couple of buckets and let them fight it out.

Little Moon gave him a nudge. "You tried this shit?" He held up a can of something called Miller Lite. "It's beer-flavored water. Here. Taste. It sucks."

Passing flaming barrels, Mickey returned to the office, routed freight toward Halifax and went downstairs to the break room armed with his Uniform Commercial Code and Macroeconomic Principles texts. At St. Peter's, finals were underway.

"That wasn't terrible," Debbie had said of the Geology exam once the blue books were turned in.

"Pangaea. Tectonic Plate Shift. Alfred Wegener. Think we'll ever use those terms again?"

"Crossword puzzles? 'Jeopardy'?"

After each exam, they met in the cafeteria, now festooned with Christmas decorations including a tinseled tree and a huge gift-wrapped carton for Toys for Tots, a program run by the unlikely alliance of the ROTC and the rock radio station.

"So?" she asked, sliding into her seat.

His American Lit final. "Fitzgerald and Hemingway: Contrast and compare."

"I was right. You went with show vs. tell, I hope."

"And you?"

"I told you," she said, pulling off her stocking cap and shaking out her hair, "there's nothing to being an English major if you love to read. 'An Introduction to Jane Austen'? I've been reading Jane Austen since I was 10."

"As an Act of Contrition, take my UCC exam."

"Oooh. Pass." She unbuttoned her coat. "What are we doing this weekend? Besides celebrating the end of the semester?" Before he could reply, she said, "Let's drive down to Belmar and walk the beach in the snow. Watch the waves."

"Too risky. The Impala is on life support." The old engine coughed and sputtered before reluctantly agreeing to turn over.

"What did the mechanic say?

Mickey had asked Bobo in the Impact shop to look at it. "He said—and I quote—'piece of shit.' Janowitz offered to steal it, set it on fire." Before Debbie could respond, he added, "I said no. Anyway, Bobo did this and that, but it'll see a junkyard before it sees the Jersey shore."

After his Macro exam—his final final—Mickey went directly to Impact, changing into his scruffy, carbon-stained Adidas and ratty flannel shirt in the parking lot, despite frigid temperatures, prickly gravel underfoot and long icicle daggers hanging from the skyway. After punching in, he found Mrs. Ada near the typewriter, writing out her Christmas cards. Broadhead gave him a dismissive glance, then buried his face in his rate book.

Mickey had the remnants of a pepperoni Blimpie in his parka pocket he intended to eat before his shift began. But Benny Luna, spotting his Impala wheeze into the lot, called him out to the dock.

"You know the marginal road coming out of Hoboken?"

Mickey said yes, he did.

"Go get Joey Baldessaro."

Mickey was puzzled. When a truck broke down, it was policy a mechanic responded. At least once a week, a box truck or a tractor came in on a hook.

"Hijacked," Luna explained. "The cops told him to call a cab."

"And...?"

"He don't want to call a cab."

Down near Hoboken, some twenty minutes away, Mickey found Baldessaro inside a phone booth, stamping his boots, clapping his gloves against his chest, rubbing his arms,

"Jesus, Mickey, you leave me out here like a fuckin' immigrant," Baldessaro said as he jumped into the Impala. "I'm fuckin' freezing." He reached over to pump the heat to high.

"You OK otherwise?" Mickey asked as he made a U-turn.

"What? The load they jacked? It ain't mine. I don't give a fuck."

"Yeah, but—"

"It was my turn. So what?"

They headed back to Jersey City. "What did they get?"

"Portable color TVs," Baldessaro told him. "Korean. But still...Merry Christmas, right? By the way, tell your old man the county cops suck. Guy wouldn't blow me a ride after he took my statement. And look at me, I'm freezing."

* * *

Hijackings were seen as a cost of doing business at Impact. They had to be inside jobs: A limited number of people knew which trucks were carrying what freight. The thieves never took down a shipment of paper products or traffic cones, but within days of the TV heist—"Heist?" Jano laughed. "Mickey, did you say heist?"—a load of mink stoles went missing. Mickey could imagine the squeals of delight when mink stoles appeared under a Christmas tree in lieu of a new ironing board, quilted robe or questionable lingerie.

Someone jacked a shipment of barber chairs.

Mickey asked Jano: "Why steal barber chairs?"

"What do they go for? Three hundred a pop? Twenty-four in the load?"

"Seventy-two hundred," said Mickey, helpfully.

"Think American Barber Supply would buy the load back for two grand?"

If neither management nor the Teamsters took precautions to prevent hijackings, it was because no one was injured when they occurred, at least not seriously. Rocco Marianna said he sprained an ankle after his load of Masonite was jacked, but the crew figured he was faking it, Rocco the closest thing to a hippie among the drivers, with his VW van with peace decals on the windshield and a Grateful Dead bumper sticker on back.

A week after he retrieved Baldessaro, Mickey was down in the lunchroom, scanning the new-car ads in the *Jersey Journal*. He heard voices from the locker room next door.

The portable TVs were for shit, said Lou Court, one of the crew.

"How's that my fault?" replied Joe Baldessaro Sr. "Did my Joey build them? No, my Joey did not build them."

Bippo said, "What do you expect for fifty bucks?"

"I expected it should work."

"Funny fuckin' thing, Lou. Mine works," Bippo told him. "Tell you what. I'll buy it back for twenty-five."

Yellow marker between his teeth, Mickey packed up quickly.

He didn't need to be seen as eavesdropping.

On Saturday, Mickey turned up at Corso's just as Sal and Mitz were closing up. He knew the end-of-the-day protocol: Too distributed the leftover loaves to the needy while Anthony was off with his pregnant wife and their daughter; Sammy was carrying much of the day's take in his pocket with the twenty-dollar bills left behind in the safe until the banks opened again on Monday. Coins would be rolled tonight and, along with the small bills, returned to the cash register tomorrow when Mitz arrived.

He knocked on the door and then waited until the Corsos exited.

"Good day, Mitz?" Mickey asked.

More detached than reserved, as if her mind was always otherwise occupied, Mitz rarely spoke. Now she shrugged her reply. She carried her purse in one gloved hand and a sack with two long loaves in the other. Her scarf was tied tight under her chin.

Corso locked the door. "Mickey, long time. How's life treating you?"

"Brrr," he said, "but otherwise fine."

"How's your girl?"

"I'm a lucky man, Sam."

"New coat? Looks sharp."

Mickey had bought a knee-length Navy topcoat and a turtleneck sweater at Robert Hall. Said his father, "It don't make you Clark Gable."

Mickey walked with the Corsos toward the two-family they shared with Anthony. "You need any help through Christmas?" he asked. "School's out."

"You volunteering?"

"Maybe I can work the counter if Mitz and Too need to go Christmas shopping."

"Ah, so four in the morning doesn't suit a man in a new topcoat."

"Any time you want, Sammy. I think I'm losing the knack, you know?"

There was a narrow path in the gray snow mound at the curb. Mickey extended his hand to Mitz to help her cross.

"You come when you want, Mickey," Sammy told him. "Maybe Mitzi wants to take the grandbaby to see Santa."

Mitz nodded in approval.

After thanks and goodbye, Mickey scooted off toward home, feeling alleviated, his troubled mind at ease.

By now, Christmas was a little more than a week away. Mickey slept in and relieved Mitz around nine o'clock. At lunch time, Too scooted out and returned with Italian cold cuts and cheese for sandwiches on warm bread. Mickey twice took the Tubes to midtown and finished his Christmas shopping at Macy's, Madison Square Garden and the Scribner Book Store on Fifth Avenue Mickey was hesitant to enter under its vaulted ceilings without Debbie as his guide. At Impact, the day office put up decorations Mickey considered mirthless, but at least they existed. Broadhead treated with contempt Mickey's question about whether he wanted to dress up their space—a little tinsel, a string of lights. Mickey thought to tell him Ed Swayback wanted it to shine like Santa's workshop, but he let it go, especially after Bippo drew a penis on the blow-up snowman on the dock.

Billy Fix pulled up in his silver Caddy just as Mickey was coming down the steps to pick up the lunch order.

With the push of a button, Fix rolled down the passenger-side window.

"Get in," he said.

The window rolled up as Mickey sat inside the warm Caddy scented by cigarettes and a woody cologne. Fix had his camel's hair coat unbuttoned.

"We got the NFL playoffs Saturday and Sunday," he said as

he handed Mickey the cache of betting slips. "Four games. They bet all four."

Mickey nodded.

"Anybody asks, talk down the Dolphins."

"Miami, right?"

"It's theirs in a cakewalk, the whole thing, so maybe put in a good word for the Raiders," Fix said. "Also, prep them for the week after Christmas. We got the NFL conference finals on the 30th and the college bowl games on New Year's Day, a Tuesday. Lots of chatter, people juiced. Boolah-boolah. We jump on it."

"Do people have money to bet after holiday shopping?"

"The wives do the shopping with what they get. The rest...The men keep themselves seeded. But you make a point, Mick. Don't let anybody in on the arm. If they don't put up, don't take the bet."

Mickey said, "But they're likely to lose..."

"If they want to borrow to bet, that's another story. Send them to me."

He paused in thought as he twirled his onyx ring.

"Maybe you want to bankroll it," Fix said. "Keep it simple. A dime on the dollar, nothing less than a hundred. Your old man won't whine."

"Ten bucks to borrow one hundred." Mickey shook his head. "No, I don't need the guys sore at me."

Fix laughed. "Better they should be pissed at me." He tapped Mickey on the thigh. "OK, kid. See you Friday."

The silver Caddy pulled away with a burst as Mickey crossed behind it toward the parking lot.

On Friday, with the betting slips and cash turned in and Broadhead rating the night's last bill of lading, Mickey put on his topcoat, collar up, and went out to see Luna. Beyond the dock, it was snowing lightly, little flakes floating from heaven. In a bright mood, Mickey recalled, with pleasure, how he, Rosemary and his mother would walk to Pershing Field, little Mickey in his rubber snap boots, and catch snowflakes on their tongues, the three of them laughing as the grass turned white. They dragged their boots as they returned home, leaving trails on the sidewalk, Mickey getting a glimpse of his mother as a girl and Rosemary happy too, her biting cynicism a few years away. Bosco and warm milk at home with Nilla wafers, the three of them at the kitchen table, tranquility before Officer Wright trudged up the stairs.

He found Luna at an empty bay, looking at the snow as it drifted past the violet streetlights.

"What do you need?" the dock boss asked.

"If you don't mind, I'm going to sneak out a little early. My girl's friends are home from college, so we're going to meet up with them. Broadhead's rating the last bill now. You should have it in ten minutes."

Sean O'Brien puttered by a forklift, a crate bound for Omemee.

Luna told Mickey to go, enjoy himself.

When Broadhead exited, Mickey grabbed the push broom and swept the carbon paper out toward the Dumpster. Then he trotted to his car, grabbed up his clothes and showered in the locker room, using his Herbal Essence shampoo. Dressed, Mickey checked himself in the mirror: black pullover and a white button-down, a new pair of navy cords, his topcoat. Debbie had teased him into parting his hair on the side and he supposed it was OK, especially since she liked it more than a little. A smile crossed his lips: Somewhere along the line, he had traded his old self in for what looked like an upgrade.

His work clothes in a bundle, plastic bottle of shampoo tucked inside, Mickey hurried to the parking lot. He;d catch up with Debbie and her friends at the Bottom of the Barrel, a brick-lined pub and restaurant below street level in Union City, about three miles away and not far from the Teamsters' office. As he plopped his clothes in the trunk, Mickey wondered if the slick roads might test the old Impala as it climbed toward the boulevard.

The Impala wouldn't start. The engine hardly protested. It groaned, coughed and went silent with a sickening wheeze.

Mickey swore. He slammed the dashboard with both palms and swore again. Sighing, he dropped his head on the steering wheel. Then he heard a knock on the windshield.

Little Moon made a circular gesture and Mickey rolled down the window.

"Dead, huh?"

"Bobo said it would hold…"

"Yeah, Bobo, he's a *stunad*. Half the time, he don't know what end of the wrench to hold."

Mickey stepped out of the car. Gravel shifted underfoot.

"So now what?" Little Moon asked. He wore a black leather coat, jeans and work boots. For some reason, he had his stocking cap in his hands. Snow gathered in his curly black hair.

"I've got to get to Union City—"

"Your girl?"

Mickey nodded.

"I knew you had a girl, sneaking upstairs to call her every night. I think I seen you on the Tubes with shopping bags, Christmas and everything."

"Moon, I gotta—"

"I'll give you a lift. No, that don't work. You want some heat after. Am I right?"

Before Mickey could reply, Moon held up a finger, turned and trotted off toward the dock.

Mickey rolled up the window. His key chain dangled from the ignition.

Little Moon returned. He tossed two keys on a ring to Mickey, who caught them against his chest.

"My old man thinks I should lend you the Red Rocket," Moon said, using his nickname for his Dodge Challenger, fire-engine red, tinted windows, mag wheels. He laughed. "My old man, huh? He's a riot."

Mickey looked at the keys.

"Take his." Benny Luna drove a big old Buick. "Drop it off by the house tomorrow. Put the keys in the mailbox."

"Let me go thank your Dad—"

"No. Go see your girl. Maybe you fill up the tank, right?"

Mickey said he would.

"You shoulda let Jano boost it, you know," Moon added, nodding toward the Impala. "Now it's just scrap."

As he dug his old clothes out of his trunk, Mickey said, "Thanks, Moon. I mean it."

"Sure you do. If we don't take care of our own, what happens next? We're all fucked."

The Buick started up with a roar.

CHAPTER EIGHT

Mickey entered the Bottom of the Barrel and walked along the pub's crowded bar toward the restaurant in back, inching by, turning sideways, "Excuse me, thanks, pardon me." There were tables for two and four along the center aisle, and they were occupied by young people mostly, college-aged, laughing, setting the world right. Through the haze, Mickey looked toward the booths—pews tucked into brick on either side of wooden tables. Holiday music played from hidden speakers: Johnny Mathis now, "Have Yourself a Merry Little Christmas."

"Mickey!"

Debbie, waving. Big smile.

They were in the corner and one of her friends had to slide out to let her wiggle past.

Debbie hurried to him. She kissed his lips.

"You look great," she said. "Very cosmopolitan."

"Should I guess who's who?"

Debbie had prepped him. He saw the girl who had been sitting next to her; Cuban, definitely, so Dolores. A journalism major at Rutgers in New Brunswick. From the aisle, he couldn't see the others. But Alice was a French major at Notre Dame, Sue an English major at Villanova outside of Philadelphia. Four Holy Family graduates who went on to Catholic colleges.

"Come on," she said, ignoring his question. She hooked his arm. "Everybody, this is Mickey."

Alice and Sue were blondes, Alice moonfaced, in a gray crocheted sweater, her hair tied back. In a suede vest over a turtleneck, Sue was sharp-featured, her hair long and straight. Sitting between them was a man Mickey placed in his mid-twenties. He had auburn hair, dark eyes behind glasses, and wore a brown corduroy blazer and a paisley shirt. Doyle lifted off his seat to shake Mickey's hand.

Mickey pointed at Alice and Sue, asking who Doyle was with. Doyle's arm went around Sue's shoulders.

Dolores slid toward the wall and tapped the bench. Mickey hung his coat on a hook as Debbie scooched in.

Lifting a pitcher of beer, Doyle filled an empty mug and passed it to Mickey.

"Cheers, mate," he said.

"Am I far behind?" Mickey asked.

"You can catch up," Dolores replied.

Mickey sipped the cold beer as Doyle stole a peanut from a bowl at the table's center. Pointing to Alice's drink, orange on top, red on the bottom, cherry on a swizzle stick, Mickey said, "What is that?"

"Tequila sunrise. Try it."

"I don't know…" He looked to Debbie, who had her a beer mug in hand.

"That's her third," she said, "and she's still upright…"

Mickey took a sip. "That is…confusing. Yeah. Er, no."

"We were waiting for you, Blue Eyes," Dolores said. "Shots?"

"Not yet," said Sue, who was staring at Mickey. "Tell us. Tell us everything."

"Sue…" Debbie warned.

"No, I like this," Sue replied. "We all know each other since grammar school. It's boring."

"We don't know Doyle," Alice said, recapturing her drink. "Who's Doyle?"

"I know Doyle," Sue replied. "But tell us, Mickey. Who are

you? And why Debbie?

Competing with the bar buzz, the conversational din, a jazz guitar played a delicate "White Christmas."

"'Why Debbie?'" Mickey repeated. "That's cake. She's the best. I mean, no offense, Sue. But it's a battle for second place."

The girls laughed. Doyle turned to Sue. "He's daring you to disagree."

"But what about you, Mickey?"

"Never been south or west of Philadelphia or north of the Ausible Chasm. Stalagmites go up from the ground, stalactites down from the ceiling. After that, it's a blur. Doyle, you're from Liverpool?"

He nodded. "Ah, the accent. Do you know many people from Liverpool?"

"Just four. Grad student at Villanova?"

"Penn Law."

"*Salute*," Mickey said, tipping his mug.

Sue said, "Mickey knows something about the law, Doyle."

"Is that so, Mickey?"

She continued, "His father's a cop. Everybody in Jersey City knows him. Officer Mike Wright."

"Enough," Debbie said. "It's not funny, Sue."

"No, no," said Mickey, "it's fine. We're all from here, right? Except Doyle, I mean. I get the subtext. How I was raised: does it wash off? I don't know, Sue."

Alice slurped the last of her drink through the swizzle stick.

"But, sure, my father's a cop. And I'm a Teamster. Maybe it's not much, but you put it together and nothing gets by us, you know?"

"Meaning?"

"Those guys on the dock, the drivers, they may not go to Villanova, but try to intimidate one of theirs and they'll send you home in a body bag."

"I certainly wasn't—"

"It's OK. Really. You're looking out for Debbie."

78

"Shots," Alice said. "We were waiting for him, remember?"

"I'll go," Sue said, easing out of the booth.

Doyle followed.

And now "Christmas Time is Here," with Charlie Brown and his gang.

"Good for you, Mickey," said Dolores, who held up a palm for him to high five.

"Mickey, what was that?" asked Debbie.

"Too much?"

"Hardly, but gee..." she replied. "Is that how you talk to the guys at Impact?"

"I guess. I guess it bled over." He took a sip of beer. "I'll apologize."

"Oh, no you won't," Dolores said. "She had that coming. Debbie, tell him."

"Sue is a little full of herself now she's bagged a lawyer—"

"'Bagged.'" Mickey laughed. "I blame myself. Next you'll be swearing. Taking the Lord's name in vain."

"Debbie? Not Debbie," Dolores said with a smile. "She's so good. But Alice? She's so bad."

"I'm so bad," said Alice, swooning.

"How is Notre Dame?" Mickey asked.

"In South Bend, I am a piece of ass."

"You are," Dolores said.

"They like 'em stocky."

"Save me," Mickey whispered.

Sue and Doyle returned empty-handed. As Doyle slid in, Sue said, "Mickey, I want to apologize. I go too far. I do. Forgive?"

They shook hands.

"Come see us over the holidays, you and Deb."

Dolores said, "I thought we were going skiing. Doe Mountain."

Debbie patted Mickey's thigh. "I'll tell you later."

"I want to be the first Cuban skier in the Olympics."

Alice said, "Where are the drinks?"

A piano and a vibraphone offered a jaunty "Let It Snow."

Laughter pealed from the bar.

"The waitress is bringing a tray," Doyle said.

Mickey, who had looked toward the laughter, saw the waitress. Snapping back, his jaw dropped. He felt an electric jolt from heels to the top of his head.

Walking purposefully, balancing six shots of tequila and lemon slices on a tray, the waitress arrived and began placing the drinks on the table. Alice reached for one, but Dolores took hold of her wrist.

"Easy, Alice," Debbie said.

Alice pouted.

The waitress scanned the group and then stopped. Amazed, she said, "Mickey?"

Mickey said, "Rosemary."

"Mickey. Jesus Christ, Mickey, you...Jesus, you're a man."

Debbie stood to let Mickey pass. He hugged his sister.

"What is going on?" Alice asked.

"Debbie," Mickey said, "this is Rosemary."

"In here, it's Jeanie," she whispered.

"'Jeanie,'" Mickey repeated.

"Hi Jeanie," said Debbie.

Rosemary Wright looked over her shoulder, then hugged Mickey again. "I get off at two," she whispered. "Meet me. And say nothing."

She looked at the group.

"Next round's on me."

"Who was that?" Doyle asked as he disturbed the drinks.

"Somebody I used to know," Mickey replied.

"I'd say she's a bit of a force."

Mickey dropped into his seat.

"To the Falcons," said Dolores, her shot glass raised.

"The Holy Family Falcons," said Sue, helpfully.

Without a lick of salt, Alice downed her drink.

* * *

Now Mickey and Debbie were Bayonne bound, driving along Kennedy Boulevard.

He had already explained: It's Benny Luna's car, the dock boss; the Impala is dead; I can't put it off any longer; Toyota dealership tomorrow morning; "want to come along?"

Mickey was wearing his filthy Adidas sneakers. On the avenue, Alice had vomited on his Hush Puppies. Dolores was charged with getting her home. Sue and Doyle were long gone.

"I can't," Debbie told him now. "I have something to do."

"'Something.'"

"Something to do with Christmas. Stop prying."

Mickey couldn't read her now. She was miffed. She was proud of the way he cared for Alice, more or less carrying her to Dolores' car, waving off her wails of apology. "I'm not a piece of ass. Nobody likes me. I'm so fat..." and another splat of vomit. But Debbie was confused by his sharp tongue. Yet she was glad he didn't let Sue push him around.

"The money, though. And your plans."

"Twenty-six hundred for a new Corolla. Manual tranny. But you're right. Any plans to move out...I have to push them back."

They were at a red light, the big Buick purring like a tiger. The snow on the blacktop had melted, but the mounds at the curb were now coated in white.

"It's wild, though. Your sister."

"Like I said. You can come." He held up the slip of paper Rosemary had passed to him. "I'd prefer it, actually."

"It's a family matter."

"Deb..."

"By the time we get back, it will be, what? Three-thirty, four o'clock. My folks would worry. They'd call hospitals."

The traffic light clicked to green.

"Mickey, the way you cut into Sue... It was a little frightening. It was almost mean. Like you were toying with her. Mickey?"

"Yeah, I was angry. Like I said, we're all from here. But now we're not as good, not worthy or whatever. Villanova. Penn Law. You know, I'm not going to be Gatsby—a guy with a mansion and English shirts and white flannel suits. I'm Jay Gatz in a torn green jersey."

"They changed you. The men at Impact. The Teamsters."

"No. That term 'wise guy'…What's it mean? Me, I'm a little wiser now. It's not a bad thing, Deb."

"Don't let them change you. You have something that can never be replaced. A soft heart. A tender heart."

Across the front seat, as big as a sofa, Debbie lay down, tucked herself into a fetal position and put her head on Mickey's thigh.

"Don't let them change you, Mickey," she murmured. "Just don't."

By the time he arrived at the Point, a diner up in Fairview some forty-five minutes from Debbie's, Rosemary was in a booth, nursing a cup of hot coffee. Before taking off his topcoat, Mickey sat next to her and hugged her tight. He kissed the top of her head.

"Go over there," she told him. "Now the Wrights hug and kiss? Jesus."

"Same ol' Roe." He tossed his coat on his side of the booth. "How many years has it been?"

"I don't count."

"How old is you, child?"

"Six. Dani is six."

"Danny. A boy."

"Danielle. A girl."

"Nothing is easy with you, is it?"

The waitress came over. Mickey ordered coffee and a piece of cheesecake. "Two forks," he said.

"Big time, Mick."

The tequila was roiling around in his stomach, yet he wasn't tipsy. Driving with the windows open helped.

"Give me your word you won't tell him."

"Will I have to? What are you doing in Union City? You don't think he might know someone who goes to that bar?"

"I needed the work. All right? A friend of mine threw me a last-minute shift."

"You haven't changed that much, Roe. He'd spot you."

She smiled. "I'm a fuckin' old lady, Mick. But nice try."

Lines around the eyes. No sparkle. She dyed her hair. Jowly. Sagging in her wraparound sweater over her waitress blouse and slacks. Worn and tired. Not yet 30 years old. He thought, *I'm looking at a stranger, but my heart is breaking.*

"What's going on? Where are you living?"

She mentioned a tumbledown town about ten miles west of the diner.

"I had you far away. California, out west. Mexico," he said. "Are you married?"

She pointed to a bare ring finger on her left hand. "But I got a guy. He's all right."

"But you need money…"

"You see a lot of homes built in the dead of winter, Mick? Right now, he's pumping gas."

"And your daughter? Do you have a picture?"

As Rosemary dug into her droopy batik bag, the waitress arrived with Mickey's coffee and cheesecake. He nudged the plate toward his sister.

She handed him a school photo. "Don't you fuckin' say it."

The shape of the face, the way she held her head, her coloring. She resembled their father. Anyone in Jersey City could tell she was Mike Wright's granddaughter.

"She's beautiful," he told her. "I'm keeping this."

She took a bite of the cheesecake. "The little things you remember. The cheesecake at the All-Star, right?"

"You loved it. As opposed to Mom's…"

"Mom could fuck up Jell-O. You still miss her? You still go

to Queen of Martyrs?"

Mickey nodded.

"You got the best of the two of them, didn't you?"

He looked away. "But I miss you, Roe."

She saw the tears in his eyes.

He said, "Mom, you...I don't have a family." He tapped his finger on Dani's photo. "My niece..."

"Mickey, come on. You know better. You can't have a family with that fuck. And look at you. You're still...Mickey, Mom loved you." She took his hand. "Don't think I didn't want to call you so many times."

Mickey tugged a paper napkin from the holder and wiped his eyes. "Sorry."

She waited. "You go to St. Peter's?"

"I do."

"Figures. Is that where you met your girl?"

He nodded and sipped the hot coffee.

"She's as cute as hell. You guys serious?"

"Could be. She's going to go for her Master's. I don't know what I'll do."

"You're working now."

"At Impact Trucking." He smiled. "I'm a Teamster."

"Ah. They got you. Don't tell me. Dad put you there."

"Nobody got me, Roe. Plus, I'm working at Corso's. I just have to figure out a few things."

Rosemary finished off the cheesecake. "Watch yourself, Mickey. Don't for a minute think you can trust him. You're sweet, but sooner or later, he's going to have to make a choice—you or the thing he wants. And he won't choose you, Mickey."

She turned to look for the waitress.

"I've got to get home. Promise me you won't tell him."

"I won't tell him."

Mickey grabbed the check. He pulled a five-dollar bill out of his pocket and put it on the table.

"Look at you. Baby Rockefeller."

"Roe, give me your address."

She stood and slipped into her down jacket.

"No, I don't think so."

Mickey stood too. "I can help."

She shook her head. "I'd rather do without than take what comes through him."

"Roe, please."

She kissed his cheek. "Goodbye, Michael Francis."

CHAPTER NINE

At the car wash, the borrowed Buick was doused with soap, slapped clean and whooshed dry. Mickey drove it over to Benny Luna's and put its keys in the mailbox, as instructed. As he walked away, he looked back to see it glisten.

Now Mickey sat alone in the finance office at the Toyota dealership. His head pounded and his stomach churned as he coped with the aftermath of tequila shots and the heartache of his sister's arrival and disappearance. He took out the picture of Dani. "Hi Dani," he said. "I'm your Uncle Mickey."

Soon, a man appeared in the musty office. He introduced himself as the general manager. Schlubby, with thick black-rimmed glasses and a sweater vest over short sleeves, he had a copy of the *Jersey Journal* in his hand.

"Tell me," he said as he sat next to Mickey, "you're Mike Wright's son. I'm right, right?"

Mickey nodded. He had said as much on the forms he filled out.

"This is outstanding," he said. "Outstanding."

He handed the newspaper to Mickey.

The banner headline read: "Drug Bust Nets 15; Heroin, Cash Found."

Little sleep challenged his reading skills. Mickey scanned the story. Jersey City Police swarmed...Marion Gardens projects. Heroin seized. A quote from Mayor Jordan. The task force, coordinated by Sgt. Michael Wright...

In the front page photo were two black men in long fur coats handcuffed together. Though the caption didn't identify him, Mickey recognized his father, in plainclothes, trailing his prisoners through early evening light, snow drifting around them. The bend in his father's nose, the snarl.

"Taking back what's ours," said the general manager. "Tell your father I said thank you."

"I will," said Mickey.

"Mr. Wright, considering and everything, I don't think we need to have your father co-sign the loan. You've made a considerable down payment. The car is on the lot. What say we close the deal now?"

The general manager held out his hand. Mickey shook it.

"Let me call Lenny back in to finalize the paperwork. I'll have them get the car ready for you. You should be out of here in under an hour."

Mickey, who had taken a bus to the dealership, thanked him again.

He entered gently, thinking his father might be sleeping. But no, Mike Wright was on the sofa, cleaning his pistol. His kit— brushes and rods, little chamois, lubricant—lay open on a bath towel.

"Congratulations," Mickey said, sealing the door behind him. "I saw the *Journal*."

He walked over and shook his father's hand. Wright looked up with suspicion.

"What's it mean?"

"We nailed some scumbags. A good night's work."

"Don't downplay it," Mickey said. "Task force. Plainclothes. You're a detective now?"

"One step at a time. It's sergeant now. Then we'll see."

"They know you know those projects."

"Like the back of my fuckin' hand." One eye closed, looking into the cylinder, he said, "They scurry like roaches when you throw the light on. Meanwhile, there's ten keys on the kitchen table. Plus thirty Gs."

"Sounds dangerous though."

"Nah. Break the first jaw you see and everybody shuts up." Wright snapped his gun shut. "Am I boring you? Take your coat off."

"Come downstairs with me," Mickey said. "I want to show you something."

"Like what? I seen snow."

"Dad, it'll take five minutes."

Wright sighed.

They stepped into the silver sunlight, Wright in his suit jacket, shoes untied.

"There," said Mickey, pointing.

"What?"

"The car. The Toyota Corolla. I bought it."

Wright frowned. He walked toward the car, circled it, blowing on his cold hands.

"How much?"

"A thousand down. Thirty-six month loan."

Wright said, "They give a kid a loan?"

"The dealer made like he was your friend."

"Ah. Now I owe."

Mickey shook his head. "Dad. Come on. I bought a new car."

"Jap. Pearl Harbor don't mean shit to your generation," he said.

"Dad, Jesus. You can't be happy for me?"

"You bought it. Don't get fuckin' carried away."

With a wave, Mickey said, "All right. Forget it." He stepped to the driver's side. "You know, I tried."

"And who buys a brown car? And standard transmission. Next week it's 1974 and you're the last guy driving stick."

* * *

And then it was Christmas.

The Olsens had their Christmas Eve ritual: tree trimming, dinner, exchanging gifts. Up early on Christmas morning to visit Warren Jr.'s grave at Holy Name Cemetery. Debbie invited Mickey to duck in and out, but he begged off.

"You're still mad at me," she said by phone. "About Sue."

Mickey had hung a wreath on his apartment door. Little needles were collecting on the carpet.

"I wasn't mad at you, so I can't still be," he said.

"We didn't even argue. Am I wrong to say what I think?"

He said no. "I agree with you. I shouldn't bring that attitude into our lives. I'll leave it on the dock."

"You have a right to fight back. Sue *was* testing you. Anyway, I want you to come to Doe Mountain."

"I can't. I'm working."

Mickey went to midnight mass at Queen of Martyrs, the collar of his topcoat turned up, a new scarf dangling, a black turtleneck, black boots, looking like Little Billy Fixx. Every pew in the church was filled. Mickey saw classmates from St. Peter's Prep and his Forensic Accounting professor, whose wife was in a wheelchair. From a distance, Mickey nodded hello. The boys' choir sang. Father Stan appeared, and the congregation rose in unison. The service was in English.

Uncertain whether he should take Communion, Mickey remained in his seat. Parishioners knelt at the altar; the host was raised. "Body of Christ." "Amen." "Body of Christ." "Amen." As the sanctified passed by, palms pressed together in prayer, Mickey silently conversed with his mother, telling her again about Dani, omitting how ground down Rosemary seemed. "Dad's fine," he told her. "You know him." He stared at the statue of the mother of Christ, who was perched on a cloud. Mickey smiled at her. Eyes fixed heavenward, she didn't respond.

He took a little drive in his Corolla, putt-putt compared to Luna's hulking V8. The horn said "excuse me" rather than "get out of the way," but that suited Mickey, who didn't want to lose his soft heart.

With the Heights tucked in for the night, he had to park six blocks from home. A cold night was growing colder. He counted the stars in the clear black sky. It's a big ol' thing, the universe, wasn't it? Somewhere out there is a place for me, he thought.

When he walked in, he found his father watching "Scrooge," a fuzzy black-and-white print, Alastair Sim. In the radiator's dry heat, Mike Wright was in his suit slacks, white shirt half-buttoned, blue socks. He had made himself some sort of drink.

He turned away from the TV. "You went to Mass?"

Mickey nodded.

"I thought about it. Be seen."

Mickey hung up his coat and scarf.

"Fix yourself a drink," Wright told him when he returned.

"No, I—Yeah, why not?"

In the kitchen, he found a big box wrapped awkwardly, but wrapped nonetheless.

"What's this?" he shouted.

"Your drink..."

Mickey poured a few fingers of J&B and dropped in an ice cube.

He joined his father on the sofa.

"Merry Christmas, Dad."

"You too."

Mickey sipped the whisky.

"You see your girl?"

"Tomorrow. They do a thing on Christmas Eve. They lost a son in Vietnam. I don't know..."

"Either they want you or they don't."

Mickey nodded, sipped again. Then he went to his room. He returned with an envelope not much larger than a raffle ticket.

"Here you go, Dad."

"Huh?"

Mickey didn't reply.

"Put on the light." Wright tore open the little envelope and found two tickets to the January 28 fight between Muhammad Ali and Joe Frazier at Madison Square Garden.

"Mickey, no…"

"You used to like the fights. Remember? You took me to the Armory that time?"

"This is no good. It's too much."

"Second promenade." Mickey pointed to the ceiling.

"Fifty a pop."

Mickey jabbed his father's thigh. "I want you to have it. OK?"

Wright slipped the tickets back in the envelope, letting them peek out of the open flap. "Go get the box in the kitchen."

Mickey hefted it against his chest and carried it into the living room.

"Hell of a wrapping job, Dad. I hate to tear it."

"Don't be a smart ass."

With the first rip of the paper, Mickey saw what it was. "A portable TV."

"For your room. Color."

Korean. Like the ones hijacked from Joey Baldessaro Jr.

"What do you think?"

"It's—" Mickey pointed to the flickering black-and-white TV, Sim quivering in his nightshirt. "I'll have color while you have—"

"It's portable, Mickey. Don't nail it down."

He pulled off the rest of the wrapping paper.

"You're not thrilled."

"No, no. It's unexpected, that's all."

"All right," Wright said, glass in hand, returning to his old TV screen. "I want to see how this ends up."

You want to see how "A Christmas Carol" ends up? Mickey thought.

"Sit. Drink."

Mickey moved the box off the table and joined his father on the sofa. The whisky was intolerable, but he sipped anyway. After a few minutes, he said, "This is nice, isn't it? Us."

"Don't get carried away, kid. If either of us had somewhere else to go, we'd be there."

At the commercial, Mickey rose and brought his glass into the kitchen.

"You're going to Corso's, right? The giveaway?"

Each Christmas morning, Sammy, Mitz and boys handed every customer a free loaf of bread, warm, fresh from the oven—a thank-you gift.

"Yep," he said, lifting the portable TV.

In the flickering blue light, Wright shrugged with mocking disinterest. Without taking his eyes from the screen, he tapped the Ali-Frazier tickets. "Still. You done it right. Smart.

"I'll tell Swayback they're from you."

Shopping bag at his side, Mickey was about to ring the bell when the door opened: Debbie in a red sweater, very festive. She kissed him on the mouth. "I love you. I do."

He chuckled. "I love you too. Merriest."

"Merriest."

When he entered, Mr. and Mrs. Olsen were waiting, Mr. Olsen in a brown button-down sweater, pipe in hand. He stepped up and clapped Mickey on the shoulder.

"We're so happy you're here, Mickey. Come, settle in."

Soon, they were in front of the tree. The room was scented by cinnamon and pine. Carols played from the stereo console.

"Warren, maybe the kids want privacy..."

"I've got nothing to hide, Mrs. Olsen. Honest. Everything is rated G." He dipped into the shopping bag and handed her a long, thin package. "Here you go."

"Did you wrap those?" Debbie whispered.

Mrs. Olsen opened the box and held up a vase, suitable for a single flower, with swirling colors.

"It's lovely, Mickey. Thank you." She blew him a little kiss.

"Mr. Olsen..." Mickey handed him his gift. A copy of Ansel Adams' first book, "Taos Pueblo."

"Good Lord. Mickey. I hope you didn't—"

"I didn't. I didn't. It's used, but in good condition. Thanks to Debbie, I have a new friend at a bookstore."

"You are thoughtful, young man," said Mr. Olsen, as he shook Mickey's hand. "What we have for you hardly seems appropriate..."

In a Christmas card, signed with love, a gift certificate for a car wash on Montgomery Avenue. Good for five trips.

Mickey laughed. "This is great, really. I love it."

"Do you?" he asked. "A young man's first car..."

"Warren," Mrs. Olsen said, "help me in the kitchen. We'll let you two be."

When they were alone, Debbie said, "You didn't spend too much, did you?"

"I swear."

"Because I didn't."

Mickey gave Debbie her first gift. A hooded Mexican rug poncho, intricate pattern, teal and gray. "For the summer in Belmar."

"Where did you—"

"You were looking at the pictures in *Sport*."

She held it up and pressed it against her chest. "I can't wait to wear it. Here, let me give you—"

"Too late." He held out another package. A framed photo.

She opened it carefully. "What is this?"

"Jane Austen's house in Chawton, Hampshire, England."

"Oh, God." She grew teary-eyed. "How—"

"Arnold at Scribner's on Fifth Avenue. We had a conversation. Same with your father's book. Pretty cool, huh?"

Debbie sprung up, kneeled on the sofa and pulled up a hidden package. "Yours," she said.

A book: "Beard on Bread" by James Beard.

"A hundred different recipes," she said. "It's new. I expect to be fed."

Smiling, nodding, Mickey flipped through the pages.

"One more for you."

A little jewelry box. He opened it and saw a small gold crucifix on a thin chain.

"Oh Deb…"

"I hope you don't mind."

He let it sit in his palm. The cross was plain, unadorned, its chain fragile. He moved his hand to let the tree lights dance on it.

"Turn it over."

On the crossbar, in block letters: Proverbs 4:23.

He said, "I don't know—"

"'Above all else, guard your heart, for everything you do flows from it.'"

They kissed tenderly.

"I do love you," she said. "I believe in you." Before he could reply, she added, "Let's not get all goopy."

Hopping off the sofa, she took up the photo of the Austen house.

"I want to show off. This is the best gift. The best."

Mickey followed her into the dining room. On the table, a bone-in ham was surrounded by sides, and plates were stacked for a buffet-style lunch. Mr. Olsen leaned against the China cabinet, engrossed in the Adams book. In the kitchen, Mrs. Olsen hummed as she opened a bottle of chilled rosé.

CHAPTER TEN

Lukasiewicz won big on the bowl games. He had Ohio State and Penn State as well as the underdogs, Nebraska and Notre Dame. Known as Tut-Tut due to his face-clenching, painful-to-witness stutter, he walked away with $325, which he let ride on the Minnesota Vikings two weeks later. At Rudy's, Mickey witnessed the bet, Tut-Tut in a shadowy booth with Billy Fixx, a rubber band around his bankroll. Mickey was at the bar to retrieve Aldo Riccardi, whose wife said she would dial the night office's number non-stop until he came home, but he couldn't help but watch Tut-Tut and Fixx, who had instructed Mickey to steer the dock crew his way if they were leaning toward Minnesota. He'd push them to bet big.

"Miami's favored by six-and-a-half," he told Mickey as they sat in his silver Caddy. "It's a tease. False fuckin' hope for Minnesota. Miami covers easy."

Miami won by 17, and Tut-Tut lost more than he had taken in on the bowl games. According to Jano, he borrowed $200 from Fixx to bump his losing bet to five-and-a-quarter plus the vig.

Mickey saw Tut-Tut slouching around the dock, but he avoided eye contact. Fixx had set him up, playing on his weakness, his willingness to believe an impulse was a strategy. It was as if the goal of the gambling operation was to dupe the crew into borrowing at ludicrous rates. Mickey made up his mind: If he was at Impact come next football season, he was going to beg off passing out the betting slips.

Now he was back at St. Peter's, the winter break over, the new semester underway. Mickey loaded up with requisites, but on Debbie's advice, signed up for an Advertising Management course. "You never know," she said. "Either way you go, you'll have to promote your services." To fulfill their science requirement, they chose Astrobiology, which, by the end of the first class, was certain to be less fun than the catalogue suggested.

"We're not going to get by watching 'Star Trek' reruns," Mickey noted.

"I blame you," she replied with neither reason nor rancor. Astrobiology aside, she had plotted a satisfying Spring: She was taking every 19th century Lit course the English department offered including one dedicated to "The Picture of Dorian Gray"—"Read it, know it, adore it," she said—and another on Anthony Trollope, who she loved.

They had found a routine: Mickey would arrive at the Olsens on Saturday in mid-afternoon; to New York most weekends, though a miserable February curtailed their long, aimless walks; museums, galleries, once a Broadway show at Mrs. Olsen's urging; back to the neighborhood for dinner, usually casual; and when the Olsens were out, not infrequently on Saturday nights, to bed, where they explored each other tenderly. On Sundays, Mickey helped out at Corso's, then hurried to Queen of Martyrs for the Latin Mass, Debbie meeting him more often than not. Then a drive in the still-new Corolla, which Debbie had failed to injure when he tried to teach her to use the stick shift, the car stalling, the gears squealing, Debbie laughing as they lurched around Roosevelt Stadium's giant parking lot. They weren't quite inseparable, but they were in love. It felt nothing like a fling.

"I want to meet your father," Debbie told him over plump, deep-fried hot dogs known as rippers at Rutt's Hut out in Clifton.

"No, I don't think you do."

"I can't make up my mind about him. In the papers, he's like a superhero."

The raids at the projects had continued. Heroin, piles of cash, arrests; one dealer jumped from a third-floor window and was impaled on the picket fence below. ""Jumped,' my balls," said Bippo. "Your father threw the nigger out the fuckin' window." Despite the violence, the residents applauded. The mayor and police chief acknowledged Sergeant Wright at press conferences.

"He's no superhero. And these days I hardly see him myself," Mickey told her.

"You fear I'll embarrass you..."

Mickey laughed. "Nice try."

"No, but really, can't we just meet? I'll come to your place."

"No, you don't want to do that either."

"Are you married?" she asked. "You must be. You have a secret life. I can't see where you live. I can't meet your family..."

"You met my sister."

"For, like, ten seconds."

"Deb, we live like two messy bachelors. His clothes are scattered like trash. I'm lucky he flushes the toilet."

"Excuses."

Mickey sighed. "OK," he said finally, "let me see when he's free."

"Soon."

"Soonish."

One Saturday afternoon, Mickey arrived at the Olsens before Debbie was ready. Mr. Olsen welcomed him into the living room. Though the temperature had climbed into the low 30s, he had a fire roaring. As he sat, he folded his newspaper and place it on the end table.

"Tell me about your bakery idea."

Mickey was surprised. Beyond their initial conversation, he hadn't mentioned anything to him about baking—neither his interest in the Culinary Institute nor his work at Corso's.

Mr. Olsen read his confusion. "The book Debbie gave you for Christmas. I asked her."

"I don't know if it's an idea. A dream, maybe?"

"Vision precedes strategy. Sequence. That's fine."

OK, thought Mickey. "Have you been in Journal Square when the PATH trains empty out?"

"Commuters by the hundreds."

"Every bakery is closed by then. Or the bread has been on the shelf for hours. And what about at one of your offices? A couple hundred people leave for the day. Where can they get fresh bread?"

Warren Olsen shrugged.

"What if there was a baker who made sure you could get product when you wanted it? Fresh product. Bread baked that afternoon."

"Bread isn't fresh at the end of the day?"

"Not the kind I'm talking about: no eggs or preservatives. Water, flour, yeast, salt. That's it. That's why the slogan works: 'Always Fresh, Just for You.'"

"I see. What about distribution?"

"A stall in the PATH station. One in the lobby of your building. You open an account or pay by credit card and you pick up your order."

"This dream of yours—how big is it? A national chain. 'Mickey's'?"

"No, no. Agatha's. That's the name."

"Your mother's name?"

"No, St. Agatha. The patron saint of bakers. But also of women who suffer breast cancer. So, there's a reference to my mom. It works all sorts of ways."

"Good."

"The other option is Honoré's."

"Ornery's?"

"Honoré's. For the French, he's the patron saint of bakers."

Mr. Olsen said, "In Paris, you see scores of people carrying home fresh bread. Baguettes."

"The name doesn't exactly roll off the tongue, though. And by the way, no national chain. Class over mass. But if Ford, GM and Chrysler want to have me set up shop in Detroit…"

"You've thought this through. I'm impressed."

Mickey smiled. "I never said it out loud before."

"It makes sense. I mean, in a general terms. Does the Culinary Institute offer management courses?"

Mickey nodded. "Several."

"What does your father say?"

"He knows my mother wanted me to graduate from St. Peter's, but we haven't talked about it lately."

Debbie was in the doorway now, coat folded over her arm.

"Would he support a transfer?" Mr. Olsen asked. "He has to know what's best for you is to move on. Jersey City is dying. Urban centers are in decay. New York can't meet its obligations. You should see Hartford, Mickey. People are fleeing."

"Dad. A little heavy for a Saturday afternoon, isn't it?"

"Perhaps," he replied, "but your Mickey is onto something. Far be it for me and all that, but he's onto something."

Mickey stood. "I'm boring your father with—"

"Not one bit," Mr. Olsen said, lifting out of his chair. "But I take your point, both of you. It's your world. Mickey, if you want to hash it out…"

"I appreciate it," he said as they shook hands.

"'Agatha's,'" Mr. Olsen repeated, as he walked them to the door.

The Corolla was parked up on the boulevard, its front bumper in a bus zone.

"What was that about?" Debbie asked.

"He's planning your future."

"*My* future?"

"No railroad flat in Jersey City for you, princess."

* * *

Mickey had possession of Impact's Polaroid camera. If a shipment came in damaged, Benny Luna would ring the office and tell him to hurry to the dock, snap a clip's worth of instant photos, carefully peel apart each one, and he and Benny would sign and date them, to the hour and minute, to testify the damage occurred en route. Mickey then put the photos in a manila envelope and delivered them upstairs. He had been instructed to put the envelope in the safe in the storage closet between the Xerox machine and the water cooler.

One mid-March night around 11, when all the trucks were in and most of the outbound freight loaded, Mickey was filing away goldenrod copies. Broadhead was long gone, departing with the *Times* and its crossword puzzle tucked under his arm.

When his busy work was completed, Mickey read his Cost Accounting text. He nibbled on Fritos he retrieved from the vending machine down in the break room.

"Mickey."

It was Jano, his dark-blue work shirt untucked late in the shift. Bippo peered around him.

"Mickey, get the camera," Jano said.

The wooden chair squeaked when Mickey turned to stand. "What's up?" He put down his book.

"Just get the fuckin' camera," Bippo said. "Hurry up."

Mickey frowned. There was no need to hurry. The scattered freight wasn't going anywhere. He unlocked the cabinet behind Broadhead's desk and withdrew the Polaroid. It was already loaded.

Jano and Bippo stepped aside as Mickey exited the office. When he turned toward the milling workers on the dock, Jano reached and grabbed the back of his flannel shirt.

"This way," he said, turning Mickey toward the stairs.

"Where are we going?"

Bippo said, "You'll see, College Boy."

As they reached the side street opposite the employee parking lot, Jano said, "Listen, Mickey. There's a car around the corner.

A yellow Oldsmobile. You can't miss it."

Mickey was confused. A driver had clipped a parked Olds? When? Incoming loads clocked in hours ago. The northbound trucks went another route toward the turnpike spur.

"You go up to the car," Jano continued, "and you're gonna see two people in the backseat."

"Fucking," added Bippo.

Jano shot him a look.

"Take the picture," Jano said. "Take as many as you can."

Mickey said, "It won't work. The flash is going to bounce off the window. You're going to see nothing but a starburst."

"Don't worry about it," Jano said. "Give it a shot."

Mickey looked at Jano. "OK..." he said finally.

He started toward the backstreet, which he already knew served as a lovers' lane, dark under the viaduct in the bowels of the city, cheaper than the cheapest motel.

Jano and Bippo were behind him. Up ahead, the yellow Olds was the only car on the block, parked a distance away from the lone working streetlight.

As he continued, Mickey saw the car was rocking. Its rear window was steamed.

He looked over his shoulder. Jano and Bippo held back; they were twenty yards away. Bippo waved him on.

Mickey readied the camera. When he drew along the car, he saw a woman, naked from the waist up, riding on a man's lap. Her skirt was hiked high and, as the man's head leaned back in ecstasy, her heavy breasts bounced in rhythm.

Even through the fog on the glass, he could see it was Councilman Swayback's wife. He remembered her from the All-Star Diner.

As instructed, Mickey snapped a photo. The flash stunned the couple, who halted in confusion.

Grabbing the first photo as it slid from the camera, Mickey shot another. Then another.

When he turned, he saw Jano and Bippo had already fled.

As the man scrambled from under the woman, Mickey grabbed the three photos.

The car door flew open.

Mickey ran as the man hoisted his pants and fixed his belt. Shouting, swearing, he raced to follow.

Mickey spun around the corner.

Jano and Bippo were waiting.

"Slow the fuck down," said Bippo.

Mickey pointing with the three photos. "He's coming," he panted.

"Just wait," said Jano. "Let him see where you go."

They left him again, strolling calmly toward the dock.

The man turned the corner.

"You motherfucker," he shouted.

Mickey ran and hurdled up the steps.

Raging, the red-faced man arrived.

Maybe ten guys from the crew were waiting.

Jano grabbed him and flung him toward the crowd. They knocked him to dock floor and began to stomp and kick him with their steel-toed boats. Blows landed repeatedly, caving skin down to the bone. No part of his body went untouched. Soon the man's arm broke, several ribs too, his knees dislocated. His nose spread across his face. The man groaned in agony.

"Please," he managed. Blood dribbled out of his ears.

"Go ahead, Jano," someone said.

Jano stepped in, reared back and threw a thunderous punch to the center of the man's face. His head striking the cement floor, the man's body stiffened, jerked and then lay useless as if dead.

Jano picked up the battered body by the shirtfront and threw him over his shoulder.

When Jano turned the corner, he discovered Swayback's wife had taken off with the Olds. He tossed the beaten man into the gutter where he would lie for hours, staring at the underbelly of the skyway.

Back at Impact, Little Moon was already hosing away the blood.

Mickey continued to watch from back near the time clock. He had seen every blow of the beating.

"Give me the pictures," Jano said, coming up behind him through the empty mechanics' bay.

"They're worthless." As predicted, nothing was identifiable behind the burst of the flash against the window.

Catching his breath, Jano glanced at them and slipped them into his pocket.

By now, Bippo had arrived. He weaved with excitement, thrilled to help execute Swayback's revenge.

Mickey stammered. "What was that, Jano?" he said, still trembling. "You made me bait."

"Nobody is gonna touch you, Mickey," Jano said, putting a hand on his shoulder. "You know that, right?"

Hanging his head, Mickey withheld his reply.

"Let it go," Jano told him. "Happens. You won't see that guy again."

"College Boy," Bippo said with a dark chortle.

Jano raised his voice. "Leave the kid alone. He stood up. He tells nobody nothing. You should come out half as good, Bip."

He turned to Mickey.

"What do you need?" Jano asked.

Mickey shook his head.

Jano clapped him on the arm.

"You done good. You done right."

Mickey sat at the typewriter as the dock went silent and the parking lot emptied. Soon he heard nothing but the click of the time clock. After a while, a siren blared up on the skyway, then vanished. Mickey looked at Broadhead's empty chair, at the silver ball of the Selectric. He took a pencil from behind his ear and put it in his shirt pocket. Falling further into himself, he saw the beating again, the blood pooling; he heard the grunts and screams, the blows landing, Little Moon whistling while he hosed down the dock.

Mickey stood and put a cover on the typewriter. He retrieved the push broom and swept the carbon paper into the corridor and delivered it to the rusted Dumpster. Then he went down to the locker room to wash up. Retrieving his books, he left Impact without punching out, his mind elsewhere.

Sickened, shocked, he drove for hours without thinking, ending up in Newark's Ironbound District, where streetlights flickered in disrepair. Next he found himself on the turnpike near the Meadowlands where they were building a stadium and a racetrack, their imposing steel skeletons in view. He headed toward bright klieg lights, where the bulldozers, excavators and graders were immobile yet threatening.

Back on a highway, he passed an empty drive-in. Ignoring signs for the Lincoln Tunnel, he made his way to Tonnelle Avenue. Now and then, from inside his little brown Corolla, Mickey relived what seemed unreal and too real—a man splayed on the dock, an ear hanging loose on the side of his head, red-bubble spittle, one eye closed. A man begging for mercy and receiving none.

High beams on the other side of the concrete divider blinded Mickey for a second or so. Little yellow and violet stars danced before his pale blue eyes.

He turned toward the Heights and parked across the street from Corso's Bakery. The hands on the clock in his dashboard told him Sammy would turn up within minutes. Wanting something good and pure, he waited.

CHAPTER ELEVEN

Mickey watched Anthony shape the high rounds. Too measured and mixed the flour for another batch of Italian loaves. Sammy was upfront, stacking the shelves, humming lightly to classical music from the old radio. Surrounded by the scent of fresh baked bread, they moved effortlessly in pursuit of their own high standards. Mickey refilled their coffee mugs and stepped aside.

He heard a rap on the back door.

Anthony looked at him. "No exceptions," he said. "Make them come back at six."

Mickey, who had flour in his hair, flour on his flannel shirt, opened the door an inch or so.

"I'm waiting for you," Mike Wright said. He wore a navy nylon jacket over a white shirt and shoulder holster. "You come home when I'm waiting for you."

Mickey stepped outside, letting the door seal behind him. "How am I supposed to know you're waiting?"

Wright stared hard at him. Then he walked away toward the mailbox at the curb. Squaring up, he said, "Get over here."

Mickey sagged. "What?"

"I heard you were there. What did you see?"

"See what?"

Wright grabbed his son's arm. "Don't fuck around, Mickey. The Olds, the Polaroids. What did you see?"

"You tell me, Dad. Tell me what I saw."

"Mickey…"

He shook free. "I didn't see anything. Except the guy. And the blood. And Swayback's wife."

"No, you didn't."

"There's about a dozen guys who can tell you you're wrong."

Wright said, "No there ain't."

"It's not going to hold, Dad. It's not. A few of those guys would eat their kids if somebody told them to. If they sense the cops will bear down—"

"Who said anything about cops? There was a fight. A guy took a beating. Nobody gives a damn. We see that shit six times a night."

"OK, then. You don't have to worry." He turned to walk away.

"Mickey. I am fuckin' talking to you."

"What works for you, Dad? That I was there, or that I wasn't? Tell me. Please. How do you want it?"

Wright stood between his son and the bakery's back door. "Are you fucking with me?"

"Careful, Dad," he said. "Maybe Eddie Swayback doesn't want anybody pushing me around."

Wright said, "Ah. You're a hard case now. No more Mommy's boy."

"Stop. I got it. I didn't see Sheila Swayback. I didn't see a guy beaten, maybe he's killed—"

"Nobody's killed. The guy's in Christ Hospital. And as far as whether she saw you, no, she didn't. Anybody else who saw you, they didn't see you. You got yourself an army of brothers behind you. You say you weren't there, they agree."

Mickey knew it was more likely they'd say he was in the middle of it, the instigator, if it could get any one of them out of a jam, but he said nothing. Mike Wright wasn't about to listen to the flour-coated boy facing him.

"Just forget about it."

"I heard you, Dad. Can I go now?"

"Yeah. Go play," Wright said.

Mickey stepped around his father and went toward the bakery.

Little Moon came to the office. He knocked hard on the door frame, ignored Broadhead, and said, "I'm going with you. On the lunch run."

Mickey was typing a manifest for a shipment of polyester tarpaulins to a sporting-goods distributor in Timmins.

"I'm all right," Mickey said, his eyes on the paperwork, the Selectric ball flying.

"Let's go," said Little Moon, snapping his fingers repeatedly.

Broadhead coughed in annoyance.

Outside, a light drizzle had returned. Mickey grabbed his hoodie from the coat tree. Little Moon wore a black T, jeans and steel-toed boots. A week had passed since the beating. No one mentioned it. If it happened, it happened somewhere else.

"We'll take mine," Little Moon said when they reached the parking lot. His red Dodge Challenger had black-leather interior. An eight ball topped the gear shift.

Gray pebbles flew as they roared toward the asphalt, thudding over a pothole.

Mickey snapped his seatbelt.

"White Mana, ain't it?"

"White Mana," Mickey confirmed.

"You eat that shit?"

"What's up, Moon?" he asked.

They left the shadows of the skyway, the muscle car running a Stop sign.

"My uncle wants me to talk to you. My Uncle Joe. Joe De-Salvo." He yanked the eight ball, sending the car racing along Newark Avenue past warehouses and empty lots. "You met him."

The Teamsters' rep. Yes, Mickey allowed. He had. They had spoken for fewer than five minutes.

Little Moon was doing fifty as they approached residential streets. Mickey was relieved at the sight of a red light up ahead.

"He likes you, my Uncle Joe." At the light, Little Moon pumped the gas impatiently, causing the engine to growl.

As the wipers slapped rain water from the windshield, Mickey watched cars and trucks soar by in both directions. He feared Little Moon was the type to dare run a red just to see if he could avoid getting T-boned.

The light clicked green, and the Challenger dovetailed as Little Moon sped into a turn onto Tonnelle Avenue toward the burger stand.

"He said you did good, my uncle. The raffle. Day-to-day. What the fuck? The guy likes you. Take the fuckin' compliment."

Transferred to Jersey City from the 1939 World's Fair in Queens, the White Mana building was a local landmark, well-lit and unmistakable. Mickey pointed toward it and Little Moon accelerated. Mickey put his hands on the dashboard. He didn't relax until they skidded into the parking lot.

"There's something for you in there," Little Moon said over the purring engine. He nodded toward the glove compartment. "Go ahead."

When he popped it open, Mickey saw a handgun not unlike his father's pistol.

"What happened to the cannon?" he asked, referring to Little Moon's Dirty Harry .44 Magnum.

"It don't fit," he replied earnestly. "But not that. Under it."

Mickey slid out an envelope that bore the insignia of the New York Knicks. Inside were two tickets, courtside seats, for the first round of the playoffs.

"Take your girl. The Knicks are the fuckin' champs, right?"

"This isn't necessary," said Mickey, who understood the tactics: Joe DeSalvo wanted to ensure his loyalty. Little Moon wanted him to see the gun. But why the effort? His father had already locked him down, telling him he had no choice but to shut up. While studying Intermediate Accounting Theory text down in the break room, Jano came in to tell him to go see Grossi, who had a load of hot UFO jeans in his trunk for sale. The crew had declared Mickey all right. One of us.

Putting the envelope in his pouch, Mickey said, "Thanks. I'll call your uncle."

"No, no. No need. You know the feds are listening, right?"

No, Mickey didn't know.

"They tapped his phones. They know we're too strong."

Mickey felt compelled to reply. "I read Hoffa's not too happy with Nixon."

"Watergate is the least of his fuckin' problems," Little Moon said, with a knowing nod. "So now you go get the burgers, right?"

Mickey put up his hood and stepped into the rain.

"You dozed off," Debbie said. "I saw you."

"Did she say 'Goldilocks'?" he asked, as they left the Astro-biology classroom.

"Goldilocks Zone. That's all you get. Stay awake."

"God, it's excruciating."

They exited Pope Hall to bright late-morning light. Debbie suggested a bench in the quad. Mickey told her he was hungry: Before he left the house, he inched his head into the refrigerator for a piece of fruit, an early peach or a plum; instead, he found a six-pack and a box of baking soda. Still miffed at his father's primordial manipulation, he thought, Fuck it. Let him fill it himself.

Off to the cafeteria, he returned with two cups of yogurt and two bananas.

"We need to decide about the summer," she told him.

It's already decided, thought Mickey as he ran a plastic

spoon through the yogurt, pulling up the fruit from the bottom. Debbie, Dolores, Alice and Sue were renting a house in Belmar, the same one they had last year, four blocks from the beach. A three-bedroom with a screened porch that held a day bed. A bungalow. A way station. They had gotten summer jobs, three as waitresses, Alice selling ice cream up and down the board-walk on a bicycle with a big ice box out front. Debbie was re-turning to a dinner shift at a seafood shack on Ocean Avenue and spending her days on the sand—lounge chair, cooler, books, radio, sunscreen. The tips were good. People who were away from it all were generous.

As for Mickey, he needed eight dollars an hour and the over-time. It provided the bridge to the future. He had to hang on as long as he could.

"We could be together every day. The beach, the sun—"

"I know. I know," he said. "But I can't. I explained."

"Mickey, how much money do you really need?"

"I don't know exactly. The Culinary Institute or whatever. I need to fatten the nest egg. The Toyota ate up the old one."

She looked to toss her banana peel. Mickey took it and tucked it into his empty yogurt cup.

"You know, Mickey, I checked. They have bakeries down the shore."

"Really?" He laughed.

"I can give you the names and numbers. I wonder if their workers wouldn't mind a little vacation. You could rotate, go place to place, filling in."

"It wouldn't be enough, Deb. I'm banking more at Impact than I'd make down there."

"It is enough, Mickey, for the summer. Come September, you'll find something new up here."

Not at eight dollars an hour. He tried a smile. "But you've got to know I want to be with you. I'm missing you already."

He could imagine a magical time. For Debbie, summers away from home meant spontaneity, freedom, a life in full. She told him little stories, all of which conveyed what she preferred: to do as she pleased, her choices her own, in the sun. Every summer day down the shore was a joy.

She stood. "So, on Fridays, I'll be on the porch looking for your headlights. We'll be together for a while and on Sundays, I'll watch you drive off toward the parkway."

He anticipated misery. When he and Debbie were apart, he slumped, he moped, he drifted; a shift at Corso's lifted him, but not for long. Never prone to insecurity, he worried nonetheless. At his worst moments, he saw their relationship ending badly: Maybe she would find somebody new without intending to, someone who was less provincial, who read and liked music, and as free as she was, who didn't have to spend his nights in purgatory with carbon paper piling up around his ankles, with cynics and malcontents who couldn't walk a straight line, who lived for theft and violence, who stood by each other but betrayed their wives, who made side bets as Little Moon shot at the panicked rats scurrying for safety at the end of the dock.

"Deb, I want to. You have to know that. But it's not possible."

"It's possible. But I understand. I do."

She gathered up their cups and spoons to walk them to the trash can. When she returned, Mickey was holding her books. She was off to Trollope, he to Intro to Law and Contracts.

He said, "I'll think about you every day. You'll be a bright, beautiful kite in the summer sky. Darting, dancing and free."

"Did you make that up? The kite metaphor?"

He shrugged. "Unless I saw it on TV."

"No, say it's yours. I like it. It's good. I'm a kite—what did you say?—'soaring in the sky.'"

"Well, it's true, isn't it?" he replied.

"So, you're the guy with the string. What? You're holding me back?"

"I didn't think of it like that, but maybe. Am I?"

"No. A kite with no string, Mickey, it flies away. It crashes.

Oooh, I do like this. Mickey, you keep me up in the sky. You keep me happy and free. I'm not going to drop from the sky. It's perfect, Mickey. Give me a kiss, Mickey. No, a kiss, not a peck…"

So now they were waiting for Mike Wright, who sent them to a place in Moonachie that served Italian. Parmigiana this and that. Veal dishes. Scampi. Mounds of linguine.

"Moonachie? A 10-mile drive?"

"You don't want your girl seen with me," Wright told him. "Not around here."

Mickey puzzled it out: The publicity surrounded the drug busts had made him a target. Benny Luna had said as much. "The *melanzana*, they're middle men," he told Mickey, using a derogatory term for blacks. "Troops. Your father better keep an eye out for who's in charge."

So now Mickey and Debbie were at a red Naugahyde booth in the Italian restaurant, quiet on a late Saturday afternoon. The bartender inspected the glasses he washed, and a waitress consolidated grated cheese, pouring the contents of one glass jar into another.

With a breadstick, Debbie nervously traced the pattern of the tablecloth. Dressed conservatively, she wore a striped sweater over a collared blouse, navy slacks, and penny loafers. Mickey teased her. "You look like a schoolteacher."

"Thanks. That's what I was going for."

Now he said, "He's past late."

"Only twenty minutes. Order something. You know you want to."

Wright came through the back door, scanned the room, and slid in next to his son. Gesturing to the waitress, he pointed to their glasses and then indicated he wanted coffee.

"You eat?" he asked.

"We're waiting for you."

"I'm not eating. But go. It's on the arm."

Mickey said, "Dad, this is Debbie Olsen. Debbie, Mike Wright."

They shook hands. "I'm glad to finally meet you, Mr. Wright."

"Mike," he said. "Yeah, this is good. This is nice."

Wright wore a gray suit, pale blue shirt, a blue-and-gray patterned tie—all of which made him look as much a cop as if he had been in uniform.

"You OK, Dad?" He seemed wired, electrified.

"Running around. But good. Sure. So, Debbie. You live in Bayonne. Holy Family, right?"

Debbie nodded.

Coffee and two fresh Cokes arrived.

He flicked a thumb at his son and an index finger at Debbie. "You been going together for a while now."

"About six months," she replied.

"He treats you right?"

"Always."

He nodded thoughtfully.

Mickey said, "Debbie's majoring in English. She wants to teach high school."

Wright took his coffee black. "And this one. Half an accountant, half a baker. But he's all right. His mother would be proud."

Mickey smiled. It was more than he expected.

"Listen," Wright said, "I gotta ask: You're not pregnant, are you?"

"Dad!"

"Jesus, Mickey. Here we are, all hush-hush—"

"You picked Moonachie."

Debbie said, "No, I'm not pregnant, Mr. Wright."

"Thank Christ," he said. "You know what we went through with his sister." He turned to his son. "My point is, you got a good thing going, you keep it that way."

"We will, Mr. Wright."

Mickey could feel his father inching out of the booth.

"Already, Dad?"

"Tick-tock. Debbie, you'll excuse me?"

"Of course."

"Mick, she's quality. A keeper. Debbie, you need anything, you call. Don't hesitate."

"Thank you."

Wright stood and took the last drink of his coffee. He reached into his jacket pocket, withdrew a thick letter-sized envelope, and slid it toward his son. "You know the routine," he said. Then he left, though not before slipping a dollar bill under his saucer and empty cup.

"What the hell was that?" Mickey said.

"He's everything and nothing like you describe him."

"I swear to you, I've never seen him like that. I think he was nervous to meet you."

Debbie held out her hand, palm side down. It quaked.

"Yeah, but you're quality," he said.

"I am quality. Am I crazy to say I liked him?"

"Probably. I don't know who that was..."

The waitress retrieved her tip. When Mickey called for the check, she told him there was none.

Debbie asked, "What's in the envelope?"

Mickey hefted it without unsealing the flap. "Raffle tickets."

CHAPTER TWELVE

Mickey found it strange that Minnow Duckett was Impact's sole black driver, given twenty percent of Jersey City was African-American and surely some of the men knew how to drive trucks. But maybe not strange. Racism ran rampant on the dock, vile slurs spat unhesitatingly to describe any African-American, whether an athlete, a musician, an actor, a politician or their fellow dues-paying Teamster.

Mickey spoke to Duck as required—a brief hello as they passed in the hallway by the time clock, selling him a raffle ticket—as did Benny Luna when he had a question about the paperwork Duck presented. But for the most part, everyone let him be. Not once did Mickey see Duck among the drivers at Rudy's on payday. Not once did Minnow Duckett ask Mickey to lie to his family. Duck tended to nod when greeted and then go on his way.

Thin with coat-hanger shoulders and skin like purple parchment paper, Duck had long crinkled fingers and endless legs that caused an awkward gait suggesting a perpetual backache. Most days, he wore a ragged red Phillies cap to hide his bald spot. Gray tufts sat above his ears.

Not long after Mickey offloaded all the raffle tickets—the new first prize a 1974 Cadillac Coupe de Ville—he arrived in the Impact lot to find Duck tilted against the hood of his car, a station wagon past its prime. His lunch pail was on its side at his feet. Approaching cautiously, Mickey saw Duck had been fighting back tears. He hesitated: Duck hadn't looked to him. But Mickey knew if one of the white workers was upset in the lot, he would've gone over to help.

"Duck," Mickey said. "Are you all right? Duck—"

Duckett swooned and began to slide off the hood. Mickey grabbed him under his arms and held him up upright.

Duck looked at him, eyes focusing slowly.

"They were going to kill me," he said plainly, a croak in his voice. "They put a gun to my head, and they were going to kill me."

"Who?" Mickey said, as Duck steadied on the hood.

"Right as I came out of the port. They cut me off, pulled me over, threw me down, put a gun right at my head."

Mickey was confused. He had never heard that a driver had been threatened, a gun pointed at him.

"Port Elizabeth?"

Duck nodded.

"What were you carrying?"

"Washing machines."

"'Washing machines'? Someone was going to kill you over washing machines?"

Duck looked at Mickey, who read his expression. The washing machines had nothing to do with it. The hijackers, who let white drivers walk away, had a chance to put down a black man.

"Who was it? Did you see?"

"The fella, he had a mask. The first fella. Like a ski mask." Duck drew a circle in front of his face. "The other fella I couldn't see. I was on the ground."

"What did the cops say?"

Pulling a handkerchief from his back pocket to wipe his face, he said, "Mr. Miglio is talking to the police."

Mickey saw no evidence of police presence—no squad car, no one tending to the victim.

"I told him—I told Mr. Miglio what happened. He told me to wait here."

Mickey said, "Duck, you shouldn't be alone out here. I'll go—"

"No, no. Mr. Miglio. I'll wait."

"Can I call home for you? Maybe someone can come and get you."

Duck said no.

"Water, maybe?"

"In broad daylight, plain as day," Duck said, looking past Mickey. "They were going to kill me. Hand to the Almighty. They were going to shoot me dead."

A Port Authority squad car pulled alongside the lot and then entered, crunching gravel. It continued slowly until it eased next to Duck.

The cop rolled down his window. He was pale and in his thirties, his blond hair in need of a trim, his manner weary, jaded. He wore short sleeves and his shirt was open at the collar, revealing he wore his white T backwards, much as Mickey's father did.

"Minnow Duckett?" said the cop. "The driver. Minnow Duckett."

Mickey now noticed the cop's partner was a woman. She was attentive, crouching to see through the windshield.

"He's Duckett," Mickey said.

"And who are you?"

"I work here." Mickey pointed toward Impact.

The cop stepped out of the car. He put his night stick back into his belt.

His partner came around back of the squad car.

As if suddenly awake, Duck said, "I'm Duckett. I'll show you my license."

"Go on," the pale cop told Mickey. "It's taken care of."

Dismissed, Mickey looked at Duck, who gave him a sad-eyed nod of gratitude.

When Mickey reached the steps to the dock, he turned toward the employee lot. The woman cop was taking notes while the other cop peered into the back of Duck's wagon, as if it were filled with washing machines.

That evening, down in the break room, as he nibbled on a drumstick over his goddamned Astrobiology notes, Mickey heard voices from next door near the lockers. Instinctively, he closed the book and cleaned up quietly, hoping to disappear without notice. But then he heard Joey Baldessaro Jr. say: "I'm telling you he saw us."

Jano hard-pressed the driver. "Don't fuck with this, Joe. Did he or didn't he?"

"I'm saying we should've put him down right there."

Bippo asked, "Why didn't you?"

Mickey stood statue-still.

"You fucked up," Bippo went on. "That's you and your brother. Fuck ups."

Mickey heard a metallic crash. Someone banged against a locker, most likely Bippo shoved sideways by Baldessaro.

"Cut it out," Jano barked. "Joey, no bullshit now: Did he see you?"

"He looked right in my fuckin' eyes. He saw our clothes. When he hit the ground, he saw our shoes. The gun, he seen it. He seen everything. I'm telling you. The fuckin' nigger, we should've put him the fuck down right there."

There was a moment's silence. Mickey thought to move, but he couldn't risk the noise.

"We're not going to lose this thing over Minnow fuckin' Duckett," Jano said finally.

"That's what I'm saying."

Bippo said, "Where's the load? The washing machines."

"Vee buried it at the place off Route 17. That ain't the issue, the washing machines."

Bippo said, 'It's an issue when Duck stands up and says it was you, you fuckin' clown."

"All right, all right," Jano said. "I'm asking you again: Did he see you?"

"How many times do I have to tell you? He made us. Eyes, clothes, shoes, the gun."

"Your voice," Bippo added.

"And that," Baldessaro conceded.

Jano said, "After we clock out, we go to the warehouse. Joey, bring Vee. But keep your father out of this. Nobody knows. You got me? Not even DeSalvo. Not yet. The four of us. That's it."

"What about Fischetti?" Bippo asked.

"We got nothing for him to move," Jano said. "Anybody asks, 'Who jacked the washing machine?' We don't know. We don't know what they're talking about. Get it, Bip?"

"I ain't the fuckin' problem," Bippo replied.

Jano told Baldessaro to wait to leave until he and Bippo were back on the dock.

As the locker room door swung open, Mickey crouched down in the windowless room, careful not to crinkle the greasy chicken sack. He heard the door squeak as it shut. Two sets of heavy boots marched along the hall toward the mechanics' bay. Then Baldessaro left. Soon, Mickey heard silence. He exited via the bay but left the property to circle around the block, traffic quaking the skyway overhead, headlights sweeping eerie warehouses down below. When he returned, no one noticed Mickey, his St. Peter's notebook and his chicken bones. Mickey saw Jano piloting a forklift, Bippo examining a cardboard crate.

It was past midnight now, closing in on one o'clock. Broadhead was gone, and the dock was silent: Only Mickey's Corolla remained in the employee lot.

Upstairs, Mickey walked past Miglio's office to Aileen

Murphy's closet-sized room, its door open wide. He went to her khaki cabinet and located Minnow Duckett's Personnel file. Mickey wrote his address in Newark and his phone number on his hand. Exiting, he was careful to ensure the cleaning crew hadn't arrived.

Back downstairs, he debated. If he warned Duck, he would be relying on him to keep a confidence. If Duck told the cops, they would press Mickey, who now knew Billy Fixx was moving items hijacked by a crew that included the Baldessaros; and Jano and Bippo were tipping off their contacts about which loads to hit.

Surely the sole black man at Impact knew how to take care of himself. Everyone suspected the hijackings were inside jobs—meaning Duck knew his fellow Teamsters had held him up and threatened him. He may have already known the specifics—that it was Baldessaro and his brother who jacked him. Joey said as much: his eyes, clothes, shoes, gun. Duck saw them all.

Leaning on the push broom, Mickey tried to reason out of responsibility. Maybe it would blow over. If Baldessaro, Jano and Bippo aren't picked up by the cops, they'd knew Duck kept quiet. They'd let it blow over. It was a load of washing machines. Insured.

Or they'd go after Duck.

Baldessaro: "We should've put him the fuck down right there."

Jano: "We're not going to lose this thing over Minnow fuckin' Duckett."

Jesus Christ: "Hear, for I will speak noble things, and from my lips will come what is right."

Mickey went to the phone on his desk. He stared at his palm.

He heard a man clear his throat. "Hello?" said Minnow Duckett from his bed in Newark.

Mickey said, "Duck, it's Mickey."

Duck made an indeterminate sound.

"From Impact," Mickey added.

Duck said, "Yes...?"

"Be careful, Duck," Mickey said. "They know you can ID them."

"Ah-um." Then he said, "They tell you to call?"

"No."

"I already spoke to the police."

"Nobody told me to call, Duck."

"Is this the threat?"

"Duck, no. I'm not—"

"Your father's that cop."

"Just watch your back, Duck."

Duckett hesitated. "Good night," he said finally.

"Good night," Mickey replied to a dial tone.

The next afternoon, Mickey turned up early, said hello to Mrs. Ada and Broadhead, put his books and a Yoo-Hoo on his desk, and opened a pneumatic tube. Duck was already in. He had been back to Port Elizabeth, retrieving a shipment of natural rubber from Mesa, Arizona, on its way to St. Mary's, Ontario, after a transfer to a northbound trailer at Impact in Jersey City.

Niagara Falls, thought Mickey, routing Duck's load.

Next, he checked the time cards. Joey Baldessaro still hadn't punched in.

On the dock, he saw nothing out of the ordinary. A few trucks were set for unloading. Long-haul trailers awaited pallets and crates. Benny Luna was in his booth and the crew slouched nearby, awaiting the four o'clock buzzer. The scent of gas fumes and motor oil hung in the sticky air. Coming up the steps, pushing his hands into his gloves, Jano bumped against Mickey, a playful nudge. Mickey walked off before checking to see if Bippo looked at him sideways.

The day had been endless. Mickey had slept poorly; and when his father came in, he buried his face in his pillow. At St. Peter's, classes dragged on. He saw Debbie from afar: She was at a table in the cafeteria with her Trollope reading group. She gave him a little wave he returned with a forced smile that caused a frown and sad bottom lip. He indicated he would call later. On the drive to work, he decided the antidote to the morass at the Impact was more Debbie in bright sunlight. The sweet thought didn't hold.

Now Mickey went upstairs to see Louise, Miglio's secretary. She was at the copy machine.

"You got a minute?" Mickey asked.

She held up a finger, then retrieved her copies.

As if hurrying summer, Louise wore an orange floral print dress above the knee, sandals, pink lipstick, hoop earrings. Mickey followed her back to her desk, which was stationed outside Miglio's office.

In a pale yellow short sleeves, his tie at haft-mast to free his bull neck, standing, leaning on his fists, Miglio gave Mickey a quick, dismissive glance and went back to his spreadsheets.

"Who do I talk to about vacation?" Mickey asked.

"You think you get a vacation?" Louise scoffed.

"I've been here a year."

"Not really," she replied as she sat, her skirt hiking higher.

"Almost."

"You get two weeks after a year, not almost a year," she said. "Take one."

"Does Mr. Broadhead sign off?"

"Tell him. He'll have to route. We can bring in a temp to type."

Mickey said thanks.

"Don't tell him until the last minute," she added. "Nobody wants to listen to him whine."

Back downstairs, he found Joey Baldessaro in the office, hunched over the adding machine. To Broadhead's annoyance, he had put his lunch pail on his desk.

Mickey stopped. Throughout the afternoon, he had practiced a breezy, offhanded tone in case he felt the weight of suspicion from Jano or Bippo. He slipped into his chair without comment.

The driver examined his tally. He crumbled the slip of paper and tossed it on the floor as he walked to the door.

"Joey," Mickey said, pointing. "Your lunch pail."

"I'd lose my fuckin' head if it wasn't attached," he muttered, pivoting it to retrieve it.

Broadhead gave it a nudge with his pen.

Mickey delivered sacks of burgers and fries to the wooden reel outside Luna's dock. The lunch whistle blew. Hand trucks dropped with metallic clatter, forklifts wheezed to a halt. The warmer weather freeing them from gathering around a barrel fire or huddling inside a truck, the men used crates as tabletops. Mickey stepped aside as they collected their food or snapped open their lunch pails. Then he headed back toward the office.

"Mickey."

He turned.

"What's on your mind?" Jano asked. "You're off in space."

Mickey shrugged.

"Where's the napkins?"

"I—"

Jano laughed. "Joking, Mick. We look like we need napkins?"

Little Moon cradled cans of cold Budweiser. He said, "Hey, Yoo-Hoo. Join."

Mickey said no.

Now he was upstairs, using the phone on Louise's desk. Before he could speak, Debbie said, "We're going to fail the final. I predict it."

Fail?

"Astrobiology. I'm serious. I mean, the requirements for planetary habitability are carbon, water, the need for a star-like sun. Why? Because that's what worked on Earth?"

"I guess."

"Here's my plan: Should a Catholic college be teaching the Big Bang Theory? And why are we relying on Soviet astronomy? Mickey... Where's the laughter?"

"I'm sorry," he said. "I spoke to Louise. I get a week. So, I can bookend it with the weekends and we can have eight full days, more or less."

"Tanfastic. But Mickey: What's bothering you? Really."

He tried to remember if he had ever lied to her. "Like I told you. Just stuff here," he replied, adding, "But, sure, let's go with Genesis on the final. We'll fail, but we'll be spectacular."

"Come by tonight. I'll wait up."

"No, I'm fine."

"Are you sure?"

Nestled under covers, deep asleep, Mickey heard someone call his name.

Then he felt a light tap on his shoulder. Then a smack on his cheek.

"Mickey. Get up." Then, louder: "Mickey, wake the fuck up."

His father. A navy nylon jacket over a white T, gray slacks.

Mickey raised up on his elbows. "What?"

"Get up," Wright repeated.

"I'm up. What?"

"Tell me about this Duckett."

Alarmed, Mickey said, "What happened?"

"He's dead."

In his boxers, Mickey spun to the edge of the bed and dropped his feet on the floor.

"You were talking to him," Wright said.

As he stood, Mickey saw his father was wearing his service piece in a shoulder holster under the blousy jacket.

"What happened?"

"Shot. Outside a gin mill in Newark. One in the face, one in the stomach."

"Oh, Jesus." He was awake now. "Who—Do they know who?"

"They think drive by," Wright said. "Tell me what you know."

Mickey said, "Jesus. Duck." The sky beyond the fire escape was already a soft silver-blue. 5:39 in the morning. Slipping into his old robe, he pointed toward the living room sofa.

Wright followed his son.

Mickey made a sign of the cross with his thumb atop his heart.

CHAPTER THIRTEEN

"You knew him?"

They sat on opposite ends of the sofa, Wright up on the arm.

"No, not really. He kept to himself." Mickey hung his head. His stomach lurched, his throat tightened.

"You were talking to him."

Mickey looked at his father. "I ran into him in the parking lot. He was waiting for the Port Authority cops."

"What did he tell you?"

"He was hijacked. They took his load. Washing machines."

"What else?"

"It was a real holdup. Someone pulled a gun on him."

"And? So?"

"That usually doesn't happen," Mickey said. "I never heard of it, anyway."

"Did he say who?"

Mickey hesitated. "The guy who pulled him out of the truck was wearing a ski mask. Maybe he saw his shoes. I don't know."

"What else?"

Mickey stood, walked barefoot past the coffee table and paced, hands in the robe's pocket. "What did he tell the cops?"

"Mickey, I'm asking you."

He looked at his father. He couldn't read him. "I don't know what else. What else?"

"He didn't hint at somebody? Point a finger?"

"At who? He said he didn't see who it was."

Wright ran his hand across his stubble. "You're holding back. I know you. You're holding back."

"What? He said he was scared. He thought they were going to kill him. And you're saying they did."

"No. No. I did not. I'm asking what you know."

"Why you?" Mickey asked. "They shot him in Newark."

Wright glared at him. Then he said, "DeSalvo needs to know. That is, if it fuckin' suits you, Mickey. Otherwise, you don't want to be anywhere near this thing. You hear me? If they come to talk to you, let me know before you say word one."

"Who's 'they'?"

"Whoever. You don't say a word to nobody. Including that girlfriend of yours. If she sees in the papers a guy from Impact got put down, you say you don't know."

"Of course I know."

"Then you say 'A guy I know got killed.' Then move on. Put a tight lid on this, Mickey. I don't care if it's the FBI—"

"The FBI?" Mickey asked.

"The way it's going, they'll make this a civil rights thing if they find the shooter is white."

"Is he? Is he white?"

Wright shrugged. "Nobody seen," he told his son.

While Mickey shaved and showered, Mike Wright boiled some coffee and fried some eggs, offering neither to his son when he emerged, towel around his waist. Mickey reached under the kitchen sink, removed a rubber plunger and took it into the steamy bathroom where he unclogged the bathtub drain, completing his task with Drano. As he teaspooned the crystals into the drain, he heard his father clatter his plate and fork into the sink. He bypassed his son on the way to his bedroom. In the kitchen, Mickey looked at the mess. He left it as it was.

Wright let out a long, satisfied moan as he settled in bed. Mickey dressed. Wallet in his pocket, keys in hand, books under his arm, he left the apartment. Soon he was behind the wheel of his Corolla, parked around the corner. He put the key in the ignition. And he saw it as clearly as if he had been there: Duck leaves a bar in Newark; a car roars by and shots ring out; hit, Duck falls to the sidewalk. The bar empties; people try to tend to him. Duck moans. His blood runs toward the curb. An ambulance arrives, siren blaring, red lights spinning, but Duck is already dead, empty eyes staring at the night sky.

He wiped his eyes with the back of his wrist. Why didn't he do more? He could've let others know. A blind call to the Port Authority cops. Or the FBI.

Struggling to come to his senses, he thought to blow off his first class and drive to Our Lady Queen of Martyrs. Father Stanislaus could assure him, absolve him of his sins.

I don't deserve absolution, thought Mickey, who long ago learned he couldn't pray his way out of guilt, even for minor transgressions.

The bakery. Soon the morning rush would be over. He'd say nothing to the Corsos, but he would be comforted by the integrity of their vocation, their gentle teasing and self-deprecation, Anthony's sour diligence.

He had his Advertising Management class at nine, then directly to Cost Accounting. He wouldn't see Debbie until noon. Maybe he could find a place for his guilt by then or a way to explain his behavior. "No, I'm fine, Deb" wasn't going to work when she looked into his eyes. As he pulled the Corolla away from the curb and drove toward the boulevard, he imagined a scene: Debbie hugs Mickey; Mickey whispers and then bursts into tears.

Still, she would hold him and rock him and tell him he was a good man. "I love you, Mickey," Debbie would say.

No. She would be horrified to know he let a man die. She would know he wasn't worthy of someone as open and kind and loving as she was. Her disappointment would crush him.

"What did I do?" he said aloud. "A man is dead."

He checked the sideview mirror and maneuvered to the right lane. Turning, he drove past St. Peter's College to the gates of Holy Name Cemetery. He entered the grounds and, moving slowly, passed rows of tombstones. Men prepared a gravesite for a service. In the distance, a backhoe ripped into the earth.

By now, the sun had climbed above the skyline. The tombstones and monuments cast shadows to the west. Mickey opened a window. A cooling breeze stroked his face.

He took a bend in the gray road and, easing to a crawl, counted the trees until he found his bearing. When he arrived at his destination, he double parked, pulled the emergency brake and turned off the engine. The Corolla let out a harmless little cough.

Stepping out of the car, Mickey wiped his eyes again and ran his fingers through his hair. Though he could see the traffic on the skyway and Route 9, the cemetery was silent. He walked on the grass along a row, bypassing slate and marble tombstones, names and dates in block letters. Then he stopped.

He blessed himself and uttered a little prayer. Looking at her tombstone, he sighed and said, "Mom?"

In the quad, positioned between Gannon Hall and the cafeteria, Debbie intercepted him.

"I'm sick," he told her. "Stay back."

She put her annotated Wilde and a notebook on a bench and felt his forehead.

"No fever. But your eyes are bloodshot."

He told her he was going home to grab a nap. He would call tonight.

She had never seen him so forlorn. Something had happened.

She watched as he left the quad for the student parking lot.

Back in the Heights, he left his books in the car and picked up takeout soup from the China Jade. Up in the apartment, he pulled down a bowl and found a spoon. A rusted Brillo pad sat atop the sliver of soap in the kitchen sink.

As he poured the hot soup into the bowl, the phone rang. Let it go, he told himself. Whoever needed his father could track him down via the precinct. But then, thinking it might be Debbie, he put down the soup and lifted the handset.

"Mickey. It's Joe DeSalvo. Local 560."

He squeezed his temple with a free hand. Queasy, he sat in his father's chair.

"Mickey?"

"Yes. I'm here, Mr. DeSalvo."

Mickey heard the rush of traffic in the background. DeSalvo was in a phone booth. He remembered Little Moon's caution: The feds are listening.

"Do you need my dad?"

"I need you, kid," DeSalvo said. "Meet me. The Clam Broth House in Hoboken. You know it?"

Mickey said yes, he did.

"Twenty minutes," DeSalvo said.

"Twenty—"

DeSalvo hung up. Mickey heard coins drop.

Mickey entered the noisy bar, crowded with longshoremen from nearby piers, but didn't see DeSalvo. He shuffled across the sawdust, passing a vat of steaming clam broth for the taking, and made his way to the entrance to the adjoining restaurant. He scanned the room, stepping aside for a waitress returning to the kitchen with an empty tray. With elbows on checkerboard tablecloths, men in shirtsleeves and neckties ate fresh seafood and pasta with gusto, frosty steins of beer nearby. But no Joe DeSalvo, as far as he could see.

By now, shock receding, Mickey's head pounded. He returned to the bar and waited until the bartender noticed him.

"Have you seen Joe DeSalvo?" he asked. Though the men at the bar were all but shouting at each other, Mickey kept his voice low.

"You Wright?" the bartender asked. He had red hair and with mallet-sized hands.

Mickey nodded.

"The Erie Lackawanna waiting room," he said. Two blocks over.

"Let me have a Coke," Mickey said. He thought it might settle his stomach, give him a little boost.

The bartender wouldn't take his quarter. He said, "I'm you, I go now."

Taking his advice, Mickey drank quickly and left the quarter on the bar. Moments later, he entered the train station's majestic waiting room—global chandeliers, Tiffany stained-glass ceiling and Greek revival columns. He hesitated as he searched for De Salvo.

The Teamster boss was at a ticket booth. The man behind the bars was telling him a story. DeSalvo nodded as he listened. He saw Mickey and, throwing down his cigarette butt, told the ticket seller to hold on. He gestured for Mickey to head to a curved, pew-like bench away from a few passengers reading newspapers until their trains arrived. DeSalvo shook Mickey's hand.

"Did the feds follow you?"

Mickey frowned in confusion. "I didn't see anybody."

Agitated, he told Mickey to switch places. Now DeSalvo was in the corner, the room spread out before him.

"You heard about Duckett," he began. He wore a gray polyester suit and a green-gray tie held in place with a bar bearing the Teamsters logo. "Tell me what you heard."

"Duck was hijacked. They pointed a gun at him. Duck thought he was going to be killed."

"Who's 'they'?" DeSalvo asked. He stared into Mickey's eyes like he was trying to see what was behind them.

"The hijackers. Duck didn't recognize them. One was wearing a ski mask."

"What else?"

Mickey said, "He was scared. The Port Authority cops talked to him. Then yesterday he came in before I arrived."

"Why does he come to you?"

"I ran into him in the parking lot."

"So you didn't know him."

Mickey said no. "He kept to himself."

"Never talked to him outside of work?" he pressed.

Mickey didn't hesitate. "I barely spoke to him at work. Like I said, Duck kept to himself."

DeSalvo nodded thoughtfully. "What do you think happened?"

"Last night? I'd only be guessing."

"Go ahead. Guess."

"A coincidence. Would the hijackers go into a colored section to shoot him when they could get him when he was on the road?"

"So you're thinking separate things. One's got nothing to do with the other."

"If I had to guess…"

DeSalvo leaned in. "With the cops, you don't guess. You don't speculate. Don't volunteer."

Mickey said, "Are they really going to talk to me? Everything Duck told me, he told the Port Authority cops, right?"

"I don't know, but whatever you tell the cops, I want to know. Tell me what they ask you."

DeSalvo leaned back. He looked out toward a train that was wheezing its way into the station.

"This heat we don't need," he said. "But we take these things very serious. Remember, Minnow Duckett was a member in good standing. Doesn't matter if he wasn't on the job. He was one of us. We stand by him."

* * *

As his Corolla turned the corner, Mickey saw outside Impact two unmarked black sedans. They parked haphazardly, somehow separate but related. Entering the lot, he found a spot not far from where he had last seen Duck. He locked the car and crossed in front of the foreboding vehicles. Dressed for the air-conditioned office, he wore an old flannel over his St. Peter's Prep T. His Adidas were scarred and filthy.

As he trudged up the cement steps, he saw the crew was already milling on the dock, trailers waiting their attention. Subdued, the men watched as Mickey turned toward the office. He punched in just as the buzzer sounded down by Luna's shack.

Entering the office, he slid his Advertising Management text and notebook on his desk. Mrs. Ada was still at the IBM Selectric, typing deliberately, her paraphernalia in place.

In his seat, surrounded by his rate books, Broadhead said, "You have to go to the break room now."

Mickey saw a pneumatic tube filled with paperwork in the basket. "Let me route these—"

"They said as soon as you came in," Broadhead explained, firmly but without emotion.

Mickey nodded. Then he opened the tube. Three bills of lading. While standing, Mickey routed them: two via Mississauga, the other through Lansdowne. Then he put them in Broadhead's basket. Now Mrs. Ada would have something to do while he talked to the cops.

CHAPTER FOURTEEN

Mickey rapped on the door. At the long table where he had done his homework and eaten lunch were three men and a woman. All four wore dark suits, the men wore ties, the woman a white blouse opened a bit at the collar. Blue paper coffee cups littered the table, and the ashtrays overflowed.

Mickey ducked his head in. He said, "I'm Wright. I was told to see you." A little lilt at the end of each sentence made them sound like questions.

One of the men pointed to a chair. Mickey edged around the table. He was facing two men, ruffled, world weary. One drummed a pen on his leather notebook. To Mickey's right was the woman. Blonde with green eyes, she was big-boned, and if Debbie were here, she would say she stepped out of a Willa Cather novel. The man at the head of the table was black. He sat with military bearing, rail stiff, his suit jacket pressed and crisp.

One of the ruffled men said, "Detective Bonner, Detective Corelli. Newark PD."

The woman shook Mickey's hand. "Special Agent McKernan," she said. "This is Senior Special Agent Ward. FBI."

Ward nodded once toward Mickey.

Corelli said, "You know why we're here?"

"Minnow Duckett."

"What can you tell us about Minnow Duckett?"

Mickey wondered if they knew everything said in here could be heard in the locker room next door.

"Not much," he said. "His paperwork was clean. He came in on time. I'm sure you heard he didn't socialize."

Bonner said, "Meaning?"

"We used to say hello by the time clock."

Mickey looked at him. Bonner had an athlete's broad shoulders and a mop of blondish hair; he was shorter than Corelli, who was sinewy with a long nose. When Bonner spoke, Corelli stole glances at McKernan as she took shorthand, her notebook filled with squiggles and curls.

"Except he came to you after he was held up," Bonner said.

"That's not what happened."

DeSalvo told him: Don't volunteer.

"My mistake," Bonner said.

Mickey hadn't done a thing out of line, yet he felt trapped.

"But you were with Mr. Duckett...After," Corelli led.

"I met him in the parking lot."

"And?"

"That's it," Mickey said. "He was leaning against the hood of his car. I saw him. He seemed upset."

"Think so?" said Bonner. "So then he tells you, am I right?"

Mickey nodded. "He said he was hijacked coming out of Port Elizabeth. They threw him on the ground."

"'They,'" said Corelli.

"One wore a ski mask, Duck said."

"What else?"

"If he recognized either of them, he didn't tell me."

Mickey was talking now to whoever was eavesdropping in the locker room. He remembered not what Duck had told him, but what Baldessaro had said: "He looked right into my eyes. He saw our clothes. He saw our shoes. The gun. He saw everything."

"In your job," said Bonner, "do you have reason to know personal details about the drivers?"

135

Mickey shook his head.

"So you didn't know where Mr. Duckett lived."

"No," Now Mickey wondered if they knew he had gone into Murphy's files.

"Anybody ask you where he lived?" Bonner asked.

Mickey said no.

"Anybody ask you anything about him?"

Mickey thought for a moment. His father had asked him. So did DeSalvo. But no one on the dock had.

"My father," Mickey said. "He's a cop. Jersey City. We were talking over breakfast this morning."

Corelli looked at his partner.

"Before this morning?" Bonner said.

Mickey frowned. "My father? No. Why?"

No one answered his question.

"Just be clear," Corelli said, "Mr. Duckett sees you in the parking lot, and he tells you he can't recognize the men who hijacked him. Correct?"

"Correct. Yes."

"That's odd, though. To just say that."

"No, he said other things. He was scared, for instance. The gun."

Bonner said, "You're remembering…"

"No. I mean, I can tell you what he said, more or less, but the gist of it was he was hijacked, he thought he was going to be killed, and he was scared."

"And you told nobody about the conversation until you told your father," Bonner said.

"Yes sir. Nobody."

Corelli inched in. "We hear you're the one guy here who knows everybody. You get them lunch. You take a bet now and then. You collect for the raffles."

Mickey was shaken. They knew about his role in the mess with Swayback's wife, didn't they? All the blood on the dock, broken bones.

Corelli shrugged. "But we're Homicide, so, you know, who gives a fuck?"

Bonner said, "Maybe somebody does. I don't know."

Ward shifted again. He took a sip of his coffee.

"The point is," Corelli said, "this is the one guy you don't know. Yet you're the only one he tells his story to."

"Strange," Bonner said.

"Mr. Wright?" said Corelli.

"He told the Port Authority cops, didn't he? What I mean is, that's official. He could've run into anybody in the parking lot. He didn't, like, seek me out."

"So you're saying he wasn't waiting for you," Bonner said.

"Mr. Miglio told him to wait for the cops. No, he wasn't waiting for me."

They all sat in silence for a moment. Corelli lit a filtered cigarette, using a Zippo lighter with a Marine Corps insignia.

Special Agent Ward said, "Gentlemen..."

"We're good," Bonner offered. "For now."

Ward stood. He said, "Thank you, Mr. Wright."

Mickey hesitated. Then he walked sheepishly toward the door, certain he had made at least one monumental mistake, but having no clue what it was.

At a few minutes before seven o'clock, Mickey went upstairs. The day office staff was gone, their routine maintained despite the presence of the police and the FBI. Sitting on the edge of Louise's desk, he lifted the handset and dialed. A few seconds later, he heard Debbie's voice. His bones vanished and his body turned to jelly.

"Hi Deb," he said.

"What's wrong?"

"I just said hello..."

"I can feel it. What happened?"

He said, "One of the drivers was killed."

"Oh no. An accident?"

"That's the thing. They shot him. Not at work, though."

"Did you know him?"

He told her. Not well. But a bit. "A nice man. Older. Black. He kept to himself. He'd been hijacked a couple of days ago. I guess I was worried for him. I don't know…"

"I'm sorry, Mickey. Truly."

He thanked her. "So that's why I wasn't…I wasn't myself."

"Is there anything I can do?"

"No, I'll see you tomorrow. But I didn't want to dump this on you."

"Mickey—"

"And I wanted to say I'm sorry. For being so mopey, for not telling you. All this stuff…I just miss you bad, is all."

"I wish I was there to comfort you."

"You are."

"I love you, you know. Are you going to be all right?"

Probably not, he thought. "It's a shock. But, sure, yes, I'll be all right. Listen, I'll see you tomorrow. Genesis. No Soviets. Goldilocks."

"Carbon and water."

"But Deb," he added, "don't say anything to your parents. No sense dragging them into this."

"OK…"

And there was Special Agent McKernan in the corridor outside the day office.

She was taller and more formidable than she appeared in the break-room chair and now she seemed to stare through him with her green eyes.

"Senior Special Agent Ward and I believe you have more to tell us."

"I don't think so."

"About your meeting with Joe DeSalvo. The Genoveses' Joe

DeSalvo."

"I—"

"Don't. There are photos."

Mickey sagged. Then he heard himself say, "They can hear you from the locker room. In the break room. They can hear you."

She nodded thoughtfully.

"We shouldn't talk here." Mickey pointed over his shoulder. The open bay of the garage sat below them.

"You're in a precarious position," she said. "You heard Newark PD. Gambling and whatever else. They think it's leverage. So you need to work with us."

She dipped her fingers into a side pocket and came up with a business card.

Mickey read it: Nora McKernan, Special Agent, Federal Bureau of Investigation. A Newark address and phone number.

"Call in the morning. And keep this to yourself, Mr. Wright."

He said, "I have to call DeSalvo."

"Wait. It goes without saying, Mr. Wright, you can't trust Joe DeSalvo. Or any of them."

Mickey put the card in the back pocket of his jeans. "I've got to go get lunch."

"Don't use your home phone," she cautioned.

Mickey walked the dock, pencil and a menu from Monteleone's in hand. Mickey asked, then checked off roast beef, capicola and provolone, peppered ham with red peppers. Some of those grilled artichoke hearts. Don't forget the plastic forks. Get some oranges, if they got them. Payday, so the envelope outside Benny Luna's shack bulged with tens and twenties. The shack was empty, Luna and his clipboard elsewhere. Mickey stepped inside, put the bills on the table, counted and flattened them. When he made a little stack, he folded it and put it in his pocket.

The dock boss appeared. Luna took off his cap and wiped his forehead with the back of his hand. "We short?"

"No, we're good."

A spool of copper wire went by on a forklift, Henry Brodnicka driving, soaked in sweat.

"You talked to the cops."

Mickey nodded. "You?"

Luna said no. "The FBI, I heard."

Again, Mickey nodded.

"They have ideas?"

Mickey said, "I don't know what they're thinking. But they said Duck was waiting for me in the lot. That's bullshit. Miglio told him to be outside when the cops came."

"Duck told you?"

"You know, Benny, the cops told me not to say anything."

"Sure," Luna said.

"But Duck was scared shitless. They pulled a gun on him."

"Who?"

"The hijackers. And before you ask, no, he couldn't make them. He told me he saw a ski mask."

"You believed him? A colored guy?"

Mickey said, "What's the point of lying to me? Jesus, you know, Benny, I go and help a guy and the next thing here's the FBI."

Luna picked up his clipboard. "Me, I think they like to make trouble for the Teamsters."

Mickey went to the office, called Monteleone's, routed bolts of fabric to Sherbrooke, Quebec, then drove off toward Journal Square, the night air humid and oppressive, a stench rising from the sewers.

It was after one by the time he found a place to park after work. Walking along the Heights, he noticed the blue lights of TV screens behind fluttering curtains and the cracked-open windows.

The temperature was holding steady, the air still as thick as paste—July in mid-May.

His guilt was acute now: The inference behind the questions by his father, DeSalvo, Newark police, the FBI and Luna was he was involved, if only indirectly, in the murder of Minnow Duckett, confirming to him if he had he done something more than just warn, Duck would be alive. The guilt was weighing him down. On the other side of the conflict was how much damage he would do if he made his act of contrition and tried to set things right by telling the FBI about Billy Fix, the Baldessaros, Jano and Bippo. Guilt might go, but what would arrive in its place?

Up ahead, double parked outside his building, was a black Crown Vic, its lights dark but its engine purring. His father stepped out, his face a blank yet surly mask. In a gray suit and tie, Wright gave a cocky beckoning gesture with his fingers and pointed to the passenger's side. Mickey sighed.

Mike Wright waited until his son was seated before he joined him, first looking around, up the block, down the block. Pondering, he sat with his hands clutching the steering wheel. To himself, he said, "Yeah." Then the engine growled, and they leaped down the street.

"Where are we going?" Mickey asked.

Wright turned on the headlights.

"You talked to DeSalvo."

"Tomorrow. Little Moon says they tapped his phone."

"What are you going to tell him?"

Mickey said, "What the cops asked. And the FBI."

"And?" Wright ran a yellow light and turned onto Kennedy Boulevard. "You'll say what?"

"They wanted to know about Duck. Did he recognize the guys? What did he tell me? Did I give anybody his personal information?"

"What about the FBI?"

"They were observing. I don't think they said five words in

the room."

Wright zig-zagged around slow-moving traffic. "Bonner and Corelli. Did they push you?"

"How did you know—"

"Mickey, for Christ's sake. Did they push you?"

"They mentioned the raffle tickets. The football games."

"Did they ask about Billy Fix?"

"No," Mickey replied.

Looking into the rearview, Wright changed lanes, turned at the park and headed along the Western Slope, passing dense trees and at a statue of a big lazing buffalo.

"Personal information. You had it?"

Mickey hesitated. "All that stuff is sitting in a filing cabinet in the day office. Where he lives—anybody could've gotten it." He looked at the carbon smeared on his T. "It wasn't a drive by, Dad."

"They told you that?"

"They made it pretty clear they think the hijacking and Duck's murder are connected."

"Who's 'they'? The FBI?"

"Newark PD."

By now, Wright was at a red light on Tonnelle Avenue. Up ahead, the White Mana's parking lot was half-empty. A graffiti-stained U-Haul It sat near the entrance.

Wright said, "You know, the FBI…The Teamsters. This guy gets shot coming out of a bar and it's got to be the Teamsters."

He turned and took a jug handle to a road which swept into the industrial part of Secaucus, past shuttered factories and a graveyard for semis. The road was dark, the telephone poles tilting, streetlights sputtering. Mickey looked ahead and saw nothing but a ghostly water tower on the other side of the turn-pike. He shivered in fear.

"It's a dead end, Dad,"

"Oh, I know."

"Turn around, Dad."

"Mickey, somebody takes you for a ride like this, it's not good. You know what I'm telling you?"

"You're joking. Right?"

"Somebody won't be joking, Mickey. You cozy up to the FBI. Everything you do, somebody is watching."

Though the road was empty, Wright slowed down. Then he turned off the headlights. They were gliding in darkness.

"This is a lesson you get one time," Wright said, holding up a finger.

"Turn around, Dad. Put the lights on."

"You get my meaning?"

Believing he had concealed his terror, Mickey said, "I heard you."

CHAPTER FIFTEEN

While his father drifted off in front of the TV, hands drooping at his sides, Mickey tossed and turned, sat up, lay back down. Seeking solace, he slipped out of bed and removed from his wallet a black-and-white strip of photos. In the wane light, he looked at Debbie smiling, pecking his cheek, hugging him tight across the shoulders. He smiled as he remembered her scent, the warmth of her embrace, a long, stolen kiss, the two of them in their own world behind the curtain in the little booth in the Woolworth's. *Hey Deb*, Mickey thought now, *somebody sent my father to threaten me. My own father took me for a ride. Can you believe it? Right now, his gun is on the coffee table, the muzzle pointed toward my bed.*

Jaw aching from grinding his teeth, Mickey eased under the covers. He heard his father piss and wash up, then the hum of the electric razor, slap, slap, the scent of Aqua Velva. The rustle of his gear. The front door opened and closed.

The light of dawn filtered into the apartment. Mickey shut his eyes, but not for long. Rolling over provided no comfort. He padded out of bed, went into the kitchen, poured a bowl of Cheerios. The milk sour, he ate it dry. Soon he was pacing like he hadn't already made up his mind.

Dressed in yesterday's clothes, he left the apartment, walked along Summit Avenue toward Journal Square, mile-and-a-half or so, and soon he saw the morning rush in bloom: Crowded buses emptied and then filled again. Commuters marched to the PATH station for the subway to New York. Purposeful people. Briefcases. Women in heels. Busy bees. A breeze waved through.

He went to a newsstand and bought morning's *Newark Star-Ledger*. Sitting on a bench at the bus stop, he flipped through the pages until he located it: "West Ward Man Slain." He read quickly. Police are investigating a shooting. Victim identified as Minnow Duckett, 53. A truck driver. U.S. Army. Served in Italy in World War II. Widowed. Son Minnow Jr. is the owner of Duckett Auto Parts and Service. Also a veteran. Vietnam.

Mickey learned more about Duck in thirty seconds than he did working with him at Impact for going on a year. He had no idea he was a veteran, had lost his wife or had a son.

He folded the newspaper. Then he opened it again and tore out the article. The paper went in the trash can, the article in Mickey's wallet.

Leaving Journal Square, he walked along a side street, ticking past gangling trees. He was heading for the Hudson County Building, a modern charmless slab with green-tinted windows. He had been inside once before, his old Impala slapped with a parking ticket, its back bumper too close to a fire hydrant. Facing the window where he had paid the fine was a battery of phone booths, old-fashioned, tall and made of wood. The doors sealed tight.

Special Agent McKernan took down the number and called him back. "Where are you?"

Mickey told her. Then he said, "Are you bugging our home phone?"

On speaker, Senior Special Agent Ward answered. "Should we?"

Mickey didn't reply.

"Special Agent McKernan believes you have something to tell us, Mr. Wright."

Ward spoke in monotone. *Sits like a robot, speaks like a robot.* "Do you?"

"Duck didn't know who they were. Why didn't they believe that?"

"Who can answer that question, Mr. Wright?"

"They're protecting something, aren't they? Something much bigger than the cash for stolen washing machines and barber chairs."

"By 'they,' do you mean the people Mr. Duckett could not have identified?"

Mickey said, "Go see Miglio. He's got a list of every hijacking, every driver who's been jacked. Why did they think Duck was going to say something? That's not how it's done."

McKernan said, "How is it done, Mickey?"

Mickey had a row of dime laid out on the shelf beneath the pay phone. He was moving them around with an index finger. Roosevelts over here, the torches over there.

"You say nothing," he said. "You keep your mouth shut and maybe something good happens. Or something less bad."

She said, "But they suspected Duckett wouldn't go along."

"Because they pulled a gun on him. He said they were going to shoot him. They never pulled a gun on anybody else they jacked."

"Are you certain?"

Mickey hesitated. "I couldn't swear to it, no. But no one ever mentioned a gun, and I bet I talked to half the guys who were hijacked when they finally came in. Only Duck mentioned a gun."

"Do the drivers carry firearms?" Ward asked.

"If they do, they don't say. Nobody is shooting hijackers, if that's what you're asking."

Ward said, "Did Mr. Duckett run into any difficulty because he was black?"

"Ask Impact's other black guy."

"What other black guy?"

Mickey said, "There you go…"

Donnel Ward thought, *Yes, there we go.*

"You're speaking to Joe DeSalvo this morning?" McKernan asked.

"He told me to call."

"What will you tell him?"

"Your questions. You, the Newark cops…I don't know what anybody wants."

Ward said, "We'll be in touch."

"Thanks, Mickey," said McKernan.

The line gone dead, Mickey put the handset back in its cradle. He picked up another dime and, as he lifted the handset again, pumped it into the slot.

"Where are you?" DeSalvo asked.

Mickey told him.

"Why?"

"Ten phone booths. Accordion doors."

"All right. Where we met yesterday. A half hour."

"No," said Mickey, with more force than he intended. "They know. They took pictures."

"Shit." Then he said, "Wait. I'm meeting a member in good standing. A young guy we like. There's no fuckin' issue."

No issue? "I'll be walking up Summit."

"Pershing Field. By the arches."

Fifteen minutes later, Mickey was in DeSalvo's black Fleetwood Talisman, the Caddy's seats something like velvet with matching blue dashboard. DeSalvo had a cigarette going in the ashtray. Mickey was thinking, Here I am, going for another ride. Sunlight is sanctuary, isn't it?

Saying nothing about this morning's call to Ward and McKernan, Mickey reported on yesterday's interview in the break room while DeSalvo drove the avenue back toward Teamsters headquarters.

"They're going with the black thing," DeSalvo summarized. "That's how they stay in it. Like they give a fuck."

"Ward is black," Mickey offered.

"We never heard of him before yesterday. Nineteen fuckin' feds up our asses and we never heard of him."

Mickey said, "Do you think I'm in trouble?"

"You? Why?"

"The Newark cops. They mentioned I took bets. They think because I take the lunch order and did the raffle tickets I know everybody."

DeSalvo tapped ash into the tray and took another drag on the cigarette. With a push of a button, he opened the window and tossed the butt to the street.

"They might squeeze you, sure. But what do you know? You don't know nothing."

"But I actually do know something," Mickey said. "I know Duck didn't know who jacked him. I don't know how many times I can tell them that. It's like they don't believe me. But why lie? What's the point?"

"Take it easy…"

"If Duck didn't see them, why are the cops so damned sure it has to do with the hijacking?"

"I don't know, Mick. But don't fall for their bullshit." DeSalvo thought for a moment. "Not for nothing, but we had an ear in that room at Impact."

"One of the cops?"

"The locker room. Cinderblocks, but the vents. My nephew."

Little Moon. "Really?"

"Yeah, they tried to shake you, but you did good. Where's your father on all this? What's his thinking?"

"He says they're trying to pin it on the Teamsters, so be careful. They know how to set a trap."

DeSalvo nodded.

Mickey thought, *I shouldn't have said the Teamsters. I should've said us.*

"They contact you, you let me know. But don't call no more. Go see Babe, the bartender at the Clam Broth House. He'll get a message to me."

Mickey looked through the windshield. He wasn't far from home. He told DeSalvo he'd walk from here, that he had to get to class.

DeSalvo pulled the Caddy into a bus stop.

He found her in the crowded cafeteria, a big plate of French fries at her elbow, her nose in the Wilde omnibus, the Astrobabbology text tossed aside.

"That shit'll kill you," he said, pointing at her lunch.

She had seen him coming and intended to pretend he caught her by surprise. But his tone startled her.

"Excuse me, Mr. Mouth?"

"Sorry," he said as he sat. "But I'm having it worse than you. I promise."

Showered and shaved, he seemed to her much as he had been, but then again no. "How so?"

"A stupid thing with my father." He stole a French fry and dragged it through a mound of ketchup. "About poor Duck."

"You're kidding."

He told her what he could.

"All because you met in the parking lot?"

He nodded. "They are grabbing at straws."

"Clutching. Grasping. It's from Thomas More."

"Huh?"

"Never mind. I'm trying to process this."

He said, "You can't. It's insane. Let's change the subject."

"Want to split a salad?"

He returned with a Cobb salad and two Tabs.

"We're still going to Philadelphia this weekend?" she asked.

Debbie had told her parents she and Mickey were visiting Sue and her boyfriend Doyle, who had a town house. A venal sin. Mickey had booked a room at the Warwick Hotel. They were going to see the Liberty Bell, visit the art museums, eat cheesesteaks. They were getting away like grownups. For Mickey, an escape from squalor.

"I want to." He lifted out of his seat, removed his wallet and withdrew the article about Duck that had appeared in the *Star-Ledger*. As he passed it across the table, he said, "First, though, I'm going to the wake."

She read the brief story.

"It's probably on Saturday."

"I'll go with you. We'll leave from there."

"Deb—"

"Don't. I want to."

"No. It's fifteen minutes from Newark to your place. I'll drop in, then come and get you."

"Mickey, your friend is—"

"See, Deb, that's the thing. He's not my friend," he insisted. "He wasn't. I can't get them to see that. It's unbelievable." He hung his head. "I'm sorry. I'm in knots."

They ate for a while, Mickey passing his hardboiled egg across the table. The cucumber slices were fresh and crisp, as was the lettuce.

He said, "With Duck, it's an obligation, not remotely social. I was the last guy at Impact he talked to. I'll go, say a prayer and I'll come get you." He reached for her hand. "We'll have the best time in Philly."

"I hope so. We're kind of going sideways."

"Please. The last thing I need is for you to be disappointed in me."

DeSalvo entered the Briar Rose, a dusty, old-fashioned neighborhood gin mill around the corner from the Teamsters' office. The men at the bar were shrunken, defeated; they held lukewarm Bud longnecks in their fists, their eyes on the "Match

Game," silent up on a black-and-white TV. DeSalvo ignored the bartender, a tattooed woman called Pug, and walked into the cat-scented storage room.

Pug brought him over a coffee black. DeSalvo had the steaming cup to his lips when Mike Wright entered.

"What's on your mind, Joe?"

"It's like that now, Sergeant? All business?"

"The state troopers are circling Union City in broad fuckin' daylight, and the FBI is all over you guys so, you know, maybe one of those rummies at the bar is—"

"I'm looking you in the eye, Mike. Plain and simple. Your kid, he knows something."

Wright kept still. He suspected as much, even after last night's threat.

"He says the FBI's got photos of me and him. He knows that how?"

Wright shrugged. "They said so in the meet."

"My nephew says no. No photos mentioned in the interview."

"So you're saying Mickey is talking to the feds."

DeSalvo put the coffee cup on a stack of beer cartons. "I'm saying your son is talking to the feds."

Wright leaned against the sink. Dripping water dribbled toward the drain. "What could he know?"

"Loose ends. For one, he picked up Baldessaro after his brother hijacked him. Maybe he saw through the scam."

"You're telling me Baldessaro didn't sell it. Jacking himself was unnecessary. A diversion nobody bought."

"Yeah, but you took a couple of TVs." DeSalvo retrieved his coffee. "Also your boy talked to Duckett."

"So did the Port Authority cops. Duckett couldn't identify anybody."

"Maybe he tells your kid otherwise."

"No." Wright shook his head. "Mickey would've said."

"Then why is he talking to the feds?"

"If he is."

"He is," DeSalvo insisted. "Your kid...Something's up. And you shoulda seen this coming."

Wright scoffed. "Did I tell you to put the guy down?"

"Whoa! Whoa with that."

"And why pull a gun on him in the first place? Your guys made this federal, Joe. Now they're knocking on your door."

DeSalvo stood. He began to pace. "What are we going to do about it?"

"You better hope your boys don't break. A black man as vic, Joe. You handed the FBI a rainmaker."

DeSalvo sighed. "And Mickey? That's on you."

"Nobody touches him, Joe."

"If he—"

"Nobody touches him."

Notepad in hand, McKernan returned to Ward's office, an hour on the phone with the U.S. Attorney's District of New Jersey and the Department of Labor well spent. Ward directed her to a chair in front of his desk. She had taken the call in an old conference room, her forest-green blazer flung across a chair, her shoes kicked away, her feet up on a chair. But meetings with Ward seemed to demand formality, so she returned to full attire, hair brushed, lipstick reapplied, Binaca. As she sat, she looked at him and wondered how he managed to stay so neat and crisp. She'd wager his wife ironed his pajamas.

"Well?"

"Long/short: Homicide investigation is Newark's. If we want to proceed under 18 U.S.C. section 245, mazel tov. Does Washington agree?"

Ward said, "Washington agrees. With a caveat."

"Let me guess. Stay with Impact. If it goes into Local 560, back off."

Ward blinked, shook his head ever so slightly. "Not 'back

off.' Proceed with caution."

"Do you think dock workers can make the call on killing a driver without the local knowing?"

"That remains to be seen."

"I mean, shouldn't we proceed on the assumption that—"

"The most corrupt local in the history of the American labor movement would sanction the murder of a member to protect an ongoing criminal confederation."

She smiled. "They've done it before."

"In point of fact, they have not."

Now she frowned. "Not only murder. Assault, extortion, kickbacks—"

"Never a black victim. Not one. Until now."

Of course he checked, she thought. "Mr. Duckett was killed because he was black."

"We may so assert."

"On what basis?"

Ward lifted his chin and stretched his neck until it cracked. "We may very well have a witness, of a kind, to the conspiracy."

"Michael Wright Jr."

Ward said, "Yes. He is convinced the homicide is the result of the hijacking."

"And how would he know that?"

CHAPTER SIXTEEN

Mickey arrived at the funeral home, a low-slung, white-brick building on Martin Luther King Jr. Boulevard. Shining in the mid-morning sun, a gold Cadillac hearse patiently awaited its passenger. Mickey bumped his Corolla into the parking lot, taking a spot close to the sidewalk. He checked his hair and necktie in the rearview mirror and, as he stepped out, tugged on his slacks and looked down at this shined shoes.

After retrieving his blazer from the back seat, he walked to the front of the building and entered. White letters on a black sign directed him to a room at the end of a corridor, past an office and a water cooler. Mickey dusted his jacket and, stomach up in his throat, continued. He crept into the Salon C where somber organ music fanned from hidden speakers.

About fifteen people were in a room that held at least twice as many. They congregated near the closed casket, leaving a sea of empty seats. On an easel was a large framed portrait of Minnow Duckett, younger then, with a handsome woman who Mickey assumed had been his wife. Flower arrangements surrounded the casket. Mickey located a circle of lilies and red roses with a sash that read: "International Brotherhood of Teamsters," the horse-head logo on either side of the gold script.

When he stepped toward the bronze casket, Mickey felt the mourners' gazes. He was the only white person in the room.

Kneeling now, Duck an arms' length away, Mickey locked

his fingers and focused to pray. The Act of Contrition came to mind, and he began to pray not for Duck, but for himself: "O my God, I am heartily sorry for having offended thee…"

Then he heard in his mind, as clearly as if the word were spoken aloud: "I messed up, Duck. I know that. I could've called the police. I could've told Jano I heard and maybe they call it off. I know it doesn't do you a bit of good, but I'm sorry."

By now, his eyes had gone red and welled with tears. He blessed himself again. When stood and turned, the low chatter that had surrounded him stopped. Well-dressed middle-aged black men and women stared at him with curiosity and suspicion.

They know I didn't do enough, he thought. Why else would I be here?

Finally, a young man approached. Mickey saw a resemblance to Duck, but the body type was different: The young man was short, wide under his black suit jacket. When he extended his hand, Mickey saw he had his father's long fingers.

"We don't know you," he said. "I'm the son. They call me Minny."

Mickey nodded. "I worked with your dad at Impact."

"At Impact," said Minnow Duckett Jr., frowning.

"In the office. Mickey. Mickey Wright."

They migrated to the corridor.

"You knew my father?"

"Not well. But I saw him every day. I do the paperwork."

"I see," Duckett said, looking up into Mickey's eyes.

"I liked the way he carried himself. I just—I just wanted to let him know I wouldn't forget him."

"The cops talk to you?"

Mickey replied, "I'm not supposed to discuss it."

Minny Duckett slipped his arm around Mickey's waist and hurried him past another salon and into a display room of empty caskets, their lids open revealing white satin and little pillows.

"You cry for a reason," Duckett said sharply, bitterly.

Mickey shrugged.

"You know they roughed him up. Threw him on the ground and roughed him up."

Mickey nodded. "He told me."

"And then someone shoots him in the street."

"It's awful."

"Don't," Minny Duckett said. "The cops talking to you means you know something. What?"

"I know what your father told me: He didn't see who it was. That's what I know."

Duckett backed away. "Least you showed your face," he scoffed.

I'm not one of them, thought Mickey. "Like I said, I appreciated your father."

A tall, dark-skinned woman appeared. She looked at Mickey and nodded a greeting. "Minny, your uncles are here. The kids need you too."

Duckett assured her he would be but a moment longer.

"My Denise," he said. "My kids, now they have no grandfather."

"You all deserve better," Mickey replied.

"You know, I keep it simple. They catch the motherfuckers or I deal with them myself. Tell whoever you need to. I won't never let it go."

Then he thrust out his hand and said, "Thanks for coming."

He left Mickey alone among the waiting caskets.

Stepping outside, Mickey found a black sedan parked behind his Toyota. Corelli was at the wheel, Bonner in the passenger's seat.

"What are you doing here?" Corelli asked, his window open wide.

"Paying my respects."

"I thought you didn't know the guy."

"It seemed like the right thing to do."

Bonner leaned over. "Feel better now?"

Across Martin Luther King Jr. Boulevard, its engine purring as it idled, was a red Dodge Challenger with tinted windows and mag wheels.

"I said, 'Feel better now?'"

"Not really," Mickey replied. "His son is upset. Duck had grandkids. I didn't know."

"He says that a lot. Notice?" Corelli said, turning to his partner. "'I didn't know.' 'I don't know.'"

"Where to next, Mickey Wright?" Bonner asked. "Back to the FBI?"

Mickey thought to say, See that red Challenger over there... "Home, I guess."

Corelli threw the car in reverse and whipped out onto the boulevard, cutting off traffic.

Little Moon pulled away too, cautiously.

They were on the Turnpike, heading south. In a few weeks, she would be on the same road, turning onto the Garden State Parkway bound for Belmar, her summer to begin. Mickey would run in place, dirt and grime on his shoes, his bell bottoms, his soul.

"You told your mother I argued with Sue?" he said.

"Ah, he speaks." She was rooting through the collection of Motown eight-tracks tapes he'd bought: "The Temptations Greatest Hits," "The Four Tops Greatest Hits," of course Marvin Gaye's "What's Going On," Stevie Wonder's "Innervisions." "Yes, I told her. The next day. She was surprised. 'Mickey argues'? She thinks you're a saint. Why do you ask?"

"She caught me off guard. She said she thought I didn't like Sue. I think she suspects we're off on our own."

"She's more open-minded than my father," she said, lifting the Wonder masterpiece from the glove compartment.

"They have to know, Deb."

"That we're sleeping together? Of course. I said we were going to Doyle's because my father would want to know how much the Warwick costs and what did we spend on dinner…"

Mr. Olsen didn't want his daughter soiled by Teamster money. "He's not going to be happy until I'm out of Impact."

"Well, neither will you, my sweet. But, hey, we're going away for a fantabulous weekend and you're going to ravish me in a four-star hotel so I think we can dispense with thoughts of my dad."

He checked his rearview mirror again. Still no sign of Little Moon's red Challenger in the Saturday traffic.

She pushed the tape into the in-dash player. Soon, they heard funk synthesizers, the sizzle of cymbals, darting patterns on the drums and scat-singing in harmony.

"I like this one," Mickey said.

"Or course you do. Stevie Wonder is the man. The Beatles, Dylan, sure, why not? But Stevie…He's playing every instrument, you know."

Mickey fell back into his thoughts. Duck had grandkids. Mickey had only known one of his grandparents, his father's father, who also had been a Jersey City cop. He died when Mickey was six. What had that void in his life meant? How different would he have been with grandparents to love him? How will Minnie's kids…

And now Minnie, an orphan. A veteran, a hard guy who wants revenge, but an orphan. Was Minnie the kind of man who would take on the full burden of family? Mike Wright hadn't. He'd left his boy to flounder, friendless and odd, until he found a way to use him.

I could've taken the chance, could've said, "Duck, don't tell anyone you heard this from me, but it was…"

Debbie said, "Oh yeah. You're listening to Stevie."

* * *

They were out of their clothes and in the king-sized bed within minutes of checking in. Afterwards, they showered together— "My boobs are clean, Mickey..."—and soon walked hand-in-hand along Chestnut Street. The cloud of guilt that had hung over him had departed for seconds at a time. On the sunny side, they stopped at Broad Street to stare up at the statue of William Penn atop City Hall and then began to meander: the Powel House for a glimpse of an 18th century brick home; and the Athenaeum of Philadelphia, its maps, portraits and musty old books sending Debbie, until then a chatterbox, into moments of intense rumination, leaving Mickey to ponder and fret. As they zigged and zagged from Rittenhouse Square to Independence Hall, Mickey was relieved to know had Little Moon managed to find them in Philadelphia, he would have lost the trail in the congested maze.

At Independence Hall, they lingered at an exhibition honoring Sarah Franklin Bache, Benjamin Franklin's daughter. They fiddled with a glass armonica. They watched an 18th century printing press in operation. They entered a hushed room in which the Declaration of Independence and the Constitution were drafted, then walked downstairs to see the Liberty Bell. When they exited, they were greeted by a table of seniors asking visitors to sign a petition to end the Vietnam War. Over by a construction site for a new courthouse, protesters were walking in circles and waving handmade banners demanding Nixon's impeachment.

Debbie had bought a little facsimile of the first U.S. flag and a copy of Thomas Paine's "Common Sense."

"Is it corny? I don't care. I swell with patriotism," she said.

At the Olde Bar in the Old Original Bookbinder's building, they ordered Fish House Punch, a rum concoction favored by George Washington. They agreed it was awful.

Yuengling drafts in hand, figure-eight soft pretzels soon to arrive, they toasted the First Continental Congress.

"They don't make men like that anymore," she said, pointing her mug in the general direction of Independence Hall. "Don't take it personally."

Mickey smiled. "I could've done all right back then. They needed accountants. And bakers."

"School teachers, too. So we'd be fine."

"Except my mother's family was in Poland."

"Mickey Kościuszko. Brave soldier."

"Brave engineer. Kościuszko was an engineer."

"God, Mickey, you are just so much fun today…"

They went back to the hotel where, to Debbie's amusement, Mickey fell asleep atop the bedspread in his Oxford button-down and jeans. In his absence, she took a hot bath with Paine, though she had bought her Trollopes and notebooks. When she stepped out of the tub, pink and relaxed, she entered the bedroom naked. Mickey was still asleep. He woke when, wrapped in a towel, she tried to slip off his Hush Puppies.

"You grind your teeth," she said.

Mickey hardly knew where he was.

"I'll run you a bath. Clawfoot. It's fantastic. Then I'll ask the concierge for restaurants."

She let the towel drop as she walked away.

The concierge booked them a table at a chop house on Walnut Street. Downstairs in a converted bank, it seemed to Mickey what a private club might be like—black-leather banquettes with tall matching chairs, little lamps on the tables, framed paintings on the walls. The patrons' polite chatter rose over the treacly music from a player piano in the corner.

The maitre d' rotated the table to allow them to sit side-by-side and face the room. Mickey thanked him as he took his seat.

"We're the youngest people in here," Debbie whispered. "Is this what we want?"

Mickey said, "It doesn't feel like us."

"Let's leave."

Laughing at their escape, they returned to Walnut Street and then found a cavernous oyster house, casual and crowded, bright lights, white tile, lots of noise and laughter. They ordered peel-and-eat shrimp, steamers, frosted mugs of beer. When Mickey confessed he'd never had an oyster, Debbie asked the waitress for a sampler: a Big Rock, a Rose Cove, a Wellfleet. She watched as Mickey stared down at the tray.

"Which one should I try first?"

"Up to you. I don't like oysters. If I were serving a newby, I'd push the Wellfleet."

With that reminder—as if a reminder were needed—they returned to discussing their summer plans. Debbie was leaving the Friday morning before Memorial Day. Mickey had already proposed he wouldn't visit immediately; Debbie needed to settle into her routine. They would talk every night they were apart, Mickey calling the kitchen phone at the seafood shack.

"Finals and then goodbye," he summarized.

"I have to say, Mickey, I look forward, really look forward, to my summers. I'm not going to let you make it into a bad thing."

"I don't mean to. I just…It's already sad and now this with Duck and the cops. The Teamsters. On my side, it's gloomy."

"You know my opinion: walk away. You don't really need your father's permission. Shake everybody's hand and walk away."

"That's not going to make the guilt disappear."

"What guilt? Over what?"

Mickey sipped his beer. Tell her what you overheard. Don't tell her.

"I could've done more. I don't know. There are some bad guys at Impact."

"Mr. Duckett knew that too. You said they pointed a gun at him."

"I know—"

"And you don't think black people know all about what shits racists are?"

"'Shits.' Well…"

"Seriously. I don't understand why you're feeling guilty. Is it good ol' Catholic guilt? Being good and doing right isn't enough?"

"No. I just...I could've helped him."

She pushed aside the bowl of shrimp peels and took his hands.

"Mickey, what is it? What's really bothering you?"

He had gone as far as he could. Maybe if it was for the best she was leaving.

"I'm going to miss you," he said. "I guess that makes it worse. Dark, darker. I don't know."

She sat back, well aware he was concealing something from her. Smiling thinly, she watched as he reached for his beer, the cold oysters still waiting. She tried to reason, as if reason had a place in first love. Mickey was putting this terrible thing, whatever it could be, between them. He had to know keeping secrets would push them apart, more so than the distance between Jersey City and the shore. When they had promised each other complete candidness, they meant it just as much as they meant it when they said they would love each other forever. And yet he wouldn't say what's gnawing at him. He would risk their relationship to keep his secret.

His co-workers had put him in untenable situations—the gambling, the raffle tickets. She couldn't imagine what they could have done to compromise him now. But it wasn't just what they had done. Guilt implied complicity. What could he have succumbed to that would trouble him so? Look at him. He's in pain. That frown, the slump of his shoulders, his drifting pale-blue eyes.

Mickey scooped the Wellfleet from its shell. He slipped it into his mouth, chewed, swallowed.

"Well?"

"Tastes like the ocean."

"They're mild. Good for beginners."

No, he didn't like it much and washed away the aftertaste with another sip of beer. Debbie dipped a steamer into the melted butter. "Bet you these were harvested in Barnegat Bay.

My brother and I used to go out early with our pails…"

Mickey was thinking it had built to where it was now. Helping, however unwittingly, to dupe degenerate gamblers like Tut-Tut into borrowing at exorbitant rates to cover their losses; demanding $50 to support the Jersey City Democratic Party from men who needed the money for the family groceries and their kids' medical bills; Little Moon and his guns; and Swayback sanctioning the savage beating of a man who had taken his wife and how it was brushed aside by Sergeant Mike Wright, who populated his home with a portable color TV, radio, blender, vacuum cleaner, Kodak Instamatic and fifths of whiskey that were the products of hijackings and theft. All that and now Mickey concealed his knowledge of a scheme in which his fellow Teamsters had proposed killing Minnow Duckett, who is now dead.

How could he begin to tell Debbie about the man he had become? And if he really loved her, would he insist she remain at his side so she could become as soiled as he had?

"My grandmother made the best Manhattan clam chowder," she was saying. "Fresh thyme. Big chunks of potatoes…"

They made love again and afterwards, with her head on his chest, she toyed with the crucifix she had given him for Christmas. Soon, she purred to sleep and, as Mickey wriggled out from under her, she turned and nestled under the covers. Mickey put on his shirt and walked quietly to an armchair next to the wardrobe. He turned the chair, gently lifted the blinds and looked out at wisps of night clouds above the city. Two hours later, he was still there, coming to the realization he was only delaying what he knew needed to be done.

They walked across Rittenhouse Square to attend 9 a.m. Mass at St. Patrick's. Following a quick breakfast—"I'm saving myself for cheesesteaks," said Debbie—they went to the Philadelphia Museum of Art. Mickey was fascinated by Thomas Eakins:

"I never heard of this guy," he said in wonder as he stared at a painting of five doctors in a surgical theater operating on a patient whose mother recoiled nearby. Debbie went off on her own. He found her at a series of paintings by Mary Cassatt: mothers and roly-poly children in tender embrace, exuding the air of profound contentment. At the gift shop, he bought a book of photos by Paul Strand. "Give it to your dad," he said. "A gift from you." She thought to tell him he twitched in his sleep, as if he was expecting blows, but she let it pass. At the car, she tucked the book in her suitcase along with her little flag and the Paine pamphlet.

For the hell of it, Mickey ordered his cheesesteak at Geno's, Debbie hers across the street at Pat's and they met in his Corolla, each eating half of the others sandwich. They quibbled about the quality until they crossed the Walt Whitman Bridge to New Jersey. Despite the tapes in the glove compartment, they drove home to conversation, airing opinions on what would be on the Astrobiology final and "Rocky & Bullwinkle," Debbie declaring her affection for the inept Russia spy Natasha Fatale.

"Some patriot," said Mickey.

By the time they crossed the Bayonne Bridge to Kennedy Boulevard, they were mostly silent. What remained unspoken hung in the air, every now and then nudging them as if to remind them why their perfect weekend had left them downhearted with a vague sense of dread.

"Mickey, pull over."

They were on the south side of City Park. A late-afternoon softball game had drawn a crowd and, at the tennis court, a man in whites was returning serves made by a machine.

"Kiss me," she said. "Really kiss me."

They kissed and held onto each other.

"I'm not going to give up on you," she said

You should. I'm no good.

Cupping the back of his neck, she said, "Trust yourself, Mickey. I do."

You shouldn't. I'm not who you think I am. "That means everything to me, Deb."

They kissed again, and for a while, they held on tight.

CHAPTER SEVENTEEN

As obvious as a float in Macy's Thanksgiving Parade, Little Moon's red Dodge Challenger followed Mickey's Corolla to the St. Peter's College parking lot, then peeled off with a roar. From inside Gannon Hall, Mickey called Special Agent McKernan; a switchboard operator at the Federal Courthouse in Newark answered and said she would call back. Mickey read off the number of the pay phone. As the clock ticked toward the start of class, he paced: Turning up late the week before finals seemed a bad play. Then he heard the phone ring, and he scooted to answer it.

"Tell me what you were wearing when we met," he said.

McKernan did.

Her identity confirmed to his satisfaction, he said, "I thought of something. Maybe it's nothing. I don't know."

She waited.

"There's a guy at Impact. Alfred Luna. They call him Little Moon."

"Alfred Luna," McKernan repeated.

"He's related to Joe DeSalvo somehow. His father is the dock boss, Benny Luna."

"Continue," said McKernan thoughtfully.

"He's crazy for guns. He keeps one in his glove compartment, shoots at rats. He had one of those 'Dirty Harry' cannons."

"What are you thinking, Mickey?"

As if counting, he said, "He's from Impact, Duck was shot...You have the bullets from Duck's body, right?"

McKernan was at the FBI's shooting range with the newly issued Colt AR-15 semi-automatic rifle. The box magazine held twenty rounds, and she'd already been through eight of them. On the range, shells scattered like confetti at her feet.

"We'll look into this," she told him.

Good, thought Mickey as he hung up.

On Tuesday, as Mickey parked in the Impact lot, Little Moon slammed the door of his red Challenger and stormed toward him.

"You fuck," said Little Moon, who grabbed Mickey by the front of his T. "You put the cops on me."

Mickey slapped at his hand.

Little Moon shoved him. "The fuckin' FBI."

"You dumb fuck. *You* brought them in. It was *you*."

Jano trotted over. He put himself between them, holding back Little Moon with a brawny forearm.

"This fuck," Little Moon shouted, pointing around Jano, "he's meeting with the cops."

Mickey looked at Jano. "Why is he panicking? I went to Duck's wake. The Newark cops were there. They pulled me over. Meanwhile, this jackass is sitting across the street in his clownmobile. And he's been following me since. He watched me do laundry, for Christ's sake."

Little Moon spit, "The FBI—"

"Was the FBI at Duck's thing?" Mickey said. "How the fuck would I know?"

Jano turned to Little Moon. "Get going," he said firmly.

"We're onto you," Little Moon said, pointing again at Mickey.

"Moon," Jano warned.

Little Moon kicked the gravel as he walked away, joining the crew who had witnessed the tussle.

"Mick, you all right?" Jano asked. He had his work gloves in a fist. The other hand he dropped on Mickey's shoulder.

Mickey looked him in the eye. "What is with people? Duck didn't tell me anything. Why can't anybody get that through their fuckin' skulls?"

"Yeah, I know, I know. Listen, there's going to be a lot of heat around here. The cops, no. But the FBI is vicious. They got a hard-on for the Teamsters and now a colored guy is dead. Stay tight, Mickey. Remember who your friends are."

Mickey nodded.

"Little Moon throws shit, come see me. Leave Benny out of it. I'll take care of it."

"Thanks," said Mickey Wright.

Jano strode ahead, bounding up the concrete steps.

Now Mickey left a message for his father at the precinct. No emergency. Ask him to call, please. Thanks.

He did this at his desk, Broadhead listening, but pretending not to.

Mrs. Ada left without a word.

"Mr. Broadhead," Mickey began, "you might as well hear this from me. Some of those guys out there think Minnow Duckett told me something before he was killed. He didn't. I told the cops he didn't. For whatever reason, Benny Luna's son is pissed at me because the FBI talked to him. He's been follow-ing me around. Somebody told him to. Carl Janowitz says it's fine, don't worry. But, you know…" He shrugged.

Broadhead put down his pen.

Mickey said, "Whatever is going on, I just want to do my job. OK?"

Broadhead grunted.

"What?"

"Your job. What is it?"

Mickey sighed. "Believe me, I know I should've stayed right in here from the start."

"You wanted to be their friend. That was, and remains, your mistake."

Broadhead retrieved his pen.

Mickey turned onto Tonnelle Avenue, driving up to Monteleone's on the lunch run. High beams flashed in his rearview mirror and, before fear struck, he heard a single bleat from a police siren. Signaling, he eased into the parking lot of a dumpy motel, half the bulbs missing in its sign. The dark car followed.

Mike Wright stepped out and walked toward the Corolla. In his nylon jacket and slacks, he looked like a plainclothes cop who couldn't resist pulling over a wayward driver.

Mickey rolled down the window.

"You called," Wright said. "What?"

"I need to see Joe DeSalvo."

"You do, do you?"

"Something's gone wrong. Little Moon is fucking with me. The FBI called him in, and he thinks I had something to do with it."

"And why does he think that? Is it because you talk to them? They told you they knew you met with Joe down in Hoboken?"

"They told me had a photo. I told Joe."

"When did they tell you?"

"I only talked to them that night. The night after Duck was killed."

"They told you about the photo in the interview?"

"No. The women, McKernan, she pulled me aside. She wanted to be friendly. You know, with Newark threatening me about the betting. The good cop. But I told all of them what Duck said."

Wright stepped back. Headlights washed over them. He said,

"Going to the wake was dumb. Really dumb."

Mickey shook his head. "I had to. I went to Buddy Peck's father's wake. If I didn't go to Duck's, they would've thought something was up. I didn't think I'd be the only one there."

"What do you want Joe to know?"

"Just what I told you. Everything in the open."

As he watched his father ponder, he knew his lies had worked. He had practiced them as he sent freight to Etobicoke and Sault Ste. Marie, while he typed the fees Broadhead had calculated, and in the lot before he lit out for Monte's.

"They're looking for someone to blame, Dad."

Wright nodded. He rapped a knuckle on the Corolla's roof and told his son to get going.

Senior Special Agent Ward and Special Agent McKernan were at a two-seater in a coffee shop on Franklin Street. As usual, Ward had ordered tuna on toast. McKernan went with scrambled eggs. They had already gone over what Alfred Luna had told them and agreed he could be useful. Luna was bloated with unwarranted self-confidence, and he reacted poorly to pressure. Little Moon. Little Hothead, who stuttered when Ward told him failure to register for the draft upon one's eighteenth birthday was a violation of, the Selective Service Act of 1948, punishable by five years in prison, a fine of up to $50,000 or both.

"Or both," repeated McKernan as they questioned him in Impact's break room. "I say it loud, just in case anyone is eavesdropping. Again."

Now McKernan watched as Ward cut the crust from his toast. When he looked up and over her shoulder, she turned. Corelli and Bonner had entered like gunslingers. They stood on either side of the table, looking down.

"All sorts of hippies with bombs and here you are, five days a week," Corelli said, staring down McKernan's blouse.

That nose, she thought. He's a toucan. "Care to join us?"

Bonner spun the squeaky stool by the soda foundation. "We do right by our partners."

"That we do," Corelli confirmed. "Quid pro quo, though."

"A polyglot," said McKernan. "Russian too?"

"You spoke to DeSalvo's nephew," Bonner said.

"Exploratory," replied Ward, who sat at attention.

"I'll send over the notes," McKernan added.

"Summarize," Corelli said.

"He's a little shit with a lot of guns. Is he in violation of the GCA?"

Corelli looked over at Bonner.

"Gun Control Act," McKernan continued. "When the vic was hit, Luna claims he was out with a friend. At the Loop Lounge in Passaic."

"Confirmed," Ward said. "A Mrs. Yvonne Bagatini."

"A widow?" Corelli asked with a sneer.

"Hardly," said McKernan, whose eggs were growing cold. "Now you."

Bonner said, "They found Minnow's truck. Bergen County sheriffs. In a warehouse in Moonachie."

"It gets better," Corelli said. "Warehouse is rented to one Vincent Baldessaro, aka Vee, whose father and brother are employed by Impact Trucking and Transport."

Ward nodded. His perfect square of a sandwich awaited. "You'll let us know what he says."

"Of course," Bonner replied. "We do right by our partners."

"Quid pro quo," added Corelli.

"*Da svendanya*," McKernan said as she picked up her fork.

By the time Mickey arrived at Impact, there was a muted buzz on the dock. Though he didn't dare ask, he quickly found evidence of its cause: Joey Baldessaro clocked in at 3:13, about two hours earlier than usual. Joe Senior called in sick. Apparently, the FBI or Newark PD had found its way to the hijacking ring. But when he went out to Benny Luna's booth to confirm it was a Chicken Delight night, he saw Jano and Bippo at work, both moving undercounter ice machines to a trailer bound for Sudbury. They were determined, as if nothing was off.

Mickey stayed away from the break room, cleared now of law enforcement. Studying for finals, he took his Intermediate Accounting Theory text and notes out to the mechanics' bay where he sat under a bare bulb, nursing a Yoo-Hoo and snacking on a Pecan Chunky until his break ended. Back in the office, Broadhead's nose was in its rate book. Mickey noticed the adding machine was out of paper; he spooled in a new roll. Overhead, a tube rattled through the piping and landed with a dull thud. Thinking about what questions on annuities and long-term bonds might be on the exam, and rutted deep in routine, Mickey paid little attention to the arriving paperwork. He opened the plastic tube, pulled out the document and sat his desk.

The incoming load was bound for Montreal. Mickey wrote "Lansdowne" across the top of the page and, kicking through carbon paper, walked it to Broadhead's in-box. Then he noticed the description of the freight: washing machines.

Mickey dropped off the paperwork, then went to the type-writer. The moment Broadhead determined the cost, he retrieved it, typed it, pulled the ochre copy and walked the bill out to the dock. He dodged cargo and hand trucks. Walush tapped the horn as he rode by on a forklift.

Benny Luna was in his shack.

"They found Duck's load?" Mickey said as plainly as he could while handing him the bill of lading.

Looking at his clipboard, Luna nodded.

"Where?"

"Moonachie," he replied.

Luna glanced at the papers. Using a pencil he shaved with a knife, he pulled the pale-blue page and drew checkmarks next to the border crossing and the number of pieces in the load. As if Mickey wasn't there, he shouted. "Zielinski! Lansdowne. Down at five."

Allie Zielinski trotted over, reached around Mickey and grabbed the bill of lading.

"Benny?" Mickey said.

"Busy, College Boy," Luna replied as he left the shack, clipboard in his hand, pencil back up behind his ear.

Mickey stayed long after Broadhead was gone, filing away copies, tamping down his nerves. He swept the carbon paper toward the mechanics' bay, dark and silent now, then scooped up the pile with his hands. When the push broom fell, its handle slapped the concrete and Mickey jumped in fright. Eager to leave, he exited without washing up, forgetting to turn off the air-conditioner.

Stepping into the steamy night air, Mickey saw his Corolla was the only car in the lot. Digging out his key, Mickey heard the skyway moan as traffic rumbled.

He stopped. His driver's side window was gone. The passenger's side window was gone too. His seats were covered with pebbles of glass. Shot out? Easier than taking a baseball bat to it.

He opened the door and, using the edge of his notebook, began sweeping glass off the seat and onto the gravel. Next, he picked up the mat and shook it.

Now, peering over the roof of the car, he tried to imagine the bullet's trajectory. After passing through two panes of glass, how far could it go? The empty lot was coated in darkness; was it possible to find it amid the shards of gravel? There was a flashlight in Benny Luna's booth...

He pondered as headlights swept overhead.

Out of habit, he locked the car doors and then returned to Impact, bypassing the office and Luna's booth, and headed to the mechanic's bay. Mickey ran his hand along the cinderblock wall that had been chipped and pock-marked by the shots from Little Moon's .44.

"Dad," Mickey said, "Dad. Wake up."

Wright murmured and groaned. He opened his eyes slowly and, flat on his back in bed, looked up at his son.

Propping on his elbows, he muttered and coughed. "What?" he said finally.

"They shot my car. Little Moon."

Bleary, Wright coughed again. His service pistol and holster hung on a chair's rail.

Mickey walked to the living room. Stumbling, scratching the tufts of gray hair on his chest, Wright followed.

"DeSalvo's nephew is trying to throw all the attention on me—and it's working, Dad."

Wright said, "He's the only guy at Impact with a gun? Un-fuckin'-likely."

Mickey showed him a mangled bullet he picked out of the wall.

"What do you want me to do? Tell me. You talked to the FBI, you went to the funeral home."

Rubbing his eyes, Wright dropped onto the sofa in his boxers, bruised shins and bare feet.

"See, that is the kind of goody-goody bullshit your mother used to pull. 'Look at me, everybody. I'm sad. I'm decent.'" Wright pointed to the bullet. "That's your reward."

"I know what you're doing, Dad. This isn't on me. Little Moon jumps me in the parking lot. He accuses me in front of the guys. Eight hours later, I find the windows shattered."

"I told you they were gonna play hardball, right? Didn't I?"

Mickey leaned against the TV console. "Dad, pick a side, OK? Jesus. The FBI questions him and he shoots my car. Where's the gray area?"

"You don't know it was him. You don't. Look. They threat-ened you. You heard. Stay the fuck out of Newark. It's none of your business."

"DeSalvo's nephew shoots my car and it's none of my business?"

"Oh. I should go arrest him? Go beat up his old man?"

"I don't know. Be a cop. Be a father. Do something."

Wright dismissed him with a wave. "Grow the fuck up, Mickey."

"Tell me about Moonachie."

Wright inched toward the edge of his seat. "Moonachie. For Christ's sakes, what are you talking about now?"

"They found Duck's load in Moonachie."

"And?"

"Moonachie. Where you sent me to introduce you to Debbie. Ten miles from home. Did you know about the warehouse in Moonachie? How deep are you in this?"

Wright sneered. "He thinks he gets to ask questions..."

"Am I shutting up to protect you, Dad?"

Wright stared at his son. "I don't have time for his shit." Slowly, he stood. "Give me the bullet."

"I don't think so," Mickey told him.

"Mickey, you are in way the fuck over your head."

"Maybe this bullet matches what they pulled out of Duck. Maybe—"

With surprising agility, Wright sped around the coffee table and grabbed his son, putting him in a choking headlock. With his free hand, he drove a punch into his kidney and let him fall. He stomped his bare heel into his son's wrist. The bullet rolled onto the apartment floor.

Wright retrieved it as his son, on his knees, gasped and heaved.

"If you got a real brain in that fuckin' head of yours, you— Look at me. Mickey, look at me."

Mickey stood slowly. Temples pulsing, knees weak, he turned to his father.

"You never had this bullet. You hear me? Then you go do

your fuckin' job. You mind your own fuckin' business and do your job."

Woozy, Mickey stared at his father.

"I told you, Mickey. The next time, a bullet like this goes straight into your fuckin' head. You think these guys won't? Go ask your friend Duckett if they won't. A hint of a threat is all they need. They make a call and down you go."

Bullet in hand, Wright turned toward his bedroom. Mickey steadied himself on the console.

"And get the fuck out of here," Wright said, looking back. "Go to the bakery, go to your mother's church, go to your girl...I don't want to see you until you pull your head out of your ass. Go, get out."

CHAPTER EIGHTEEN

Mickey made three runs to the Corolla, stuffing his clothes—polo shirts, Ts, jeans, shorts, socks, shoes and whatnot—in an old St. Peter's Prep duffle bag he threw in the trunk. Hooking his finger on the hangers, he next brought down his dress shirts, slacks and blazer, laying them across the back seat. Finally, he retrieved his winter coats, sweaters, books and a framed fuzzy black-and-white photo of his mother as a delighted teen. What he left behind could be replaced—toiletries, his alarm clock, pencils and pens, maybe some things in the kitchen. The family photos were in a box in his father's closet. He'd have to let them go—his mother, Rosemary, birthday parties and Easter mornings were alive in his mind.

It was coming up on two in the morning. Dead time. He drove up and down the boulevard. He sat at one red light and, watching it turn green, didn't move until it went to yellow: No one came up behind him. Then, parked near the brownfields overlooking the Statue of Liberty, its copper-gone-green back turned to New Jersey, he put the driver's seat down flat and tried to sleep. His lower back ached, his wrist hurt. He stepped outside to piss and couldn't see if there was blood in the stream.

At 4 a.m., he watched from a distance as Sammy Corso opened the bakery. Too came next, then Anthony. While the front of the shop remained dark, a little light shone through from the back and Mickey could imagine them at work, happy in their routine, unfettered, doing something of merit, of worth. He could see the flour on their hands, hear the dough slap the table, feel the oven's heat. Surely they knew what kind of world surrounded them, but they succeeded in ignoring it, rising above it. They did what they wanted to the way they wanted to.

Then he stepped back in the Corolla and drove to Our Lady Queen of Martyrs, but the church was closed. The streets were silvery just before dawn.

He was in Journal Square at sun up, watching delivery trucks, milk on hand carts going into the diner. Bales of newspapers were flung toward the newsstands and candy stores. A garbage truck rumbled through and swallowed the trash flung into its yawning hatch.

He was tired of waiting now. His bank had other branches. The windows could be fixed anywhere. He had what he needed.

He drove past Holy Name Cemetery, through Lincoln Park, over the soiled Hackensack River. Over the Pulaski Skyway and, beneath it, Impact Trucking and Transport. His destination was beyond the turnpike and straight ahead. As far as he could tell, no one was tailing him.

He didn't know where the FBI kept its office in Newark, but with a phone call, he'd find out.

He was sitting in front of Ward's desk in the old courthouse when McKernan arrived. She carried her notebook and a cup of vending-machine coffee.

"We waited," said Ward.

It was maybe fifteen seconds after 9 a.m.

McKernan sat next to their visitor. "Mickey," she said with a nod. "You're looking...ragged."

Sad-eyed and slumped, Mickey didn't respond.

She put her cup on Ward's desk. "Sorry. It hasn't been easy, has it?"

Ward said, "Mr. Wright is aware the truck was located in a

warehouse rented by the Baldessaros."

"Newark still holding onto the sons?"

Ward nodded.

For some reason, Mickey noticed McKernan's pants suit matched Ward's tie.

"No," he said, "it hasn't been easy. But..."

"Go on, son," said Ward.

Invited to tell his tale, he did.

Ward said, "As you understand it, Carl Janowitz and Dominick Bippo, along with Joseph Baldessaro Jr. and Vincent Baldessaro, are the principles in a hijacking ring. Billy Fischetti moves the contraband after it's stolen."

"That's what they said."

McKernan checked her notes. They agreed with Ward's summary.

"You believe this enterprise is sanctioned by the Teamsters, by Joe DeSalvo."

"It has to be."

"Why?" Ward asked.

"Nothing happens at Impact without their approval."

Ward glanced at his deputy. The U.S. Attorney's office made them aware Vincent Miglio, Impact's general manager, had paid the local $17,000 for "labor peace." It wasn't a far leap to think he allowed the Teamsters to profit from goods stolen from his company's trucks.

"Did they mention DeSalvo?" he asked.

"They said leave him out of it."

"Out of what, Mr. Wright?"

He shrugged. "Whatever plans they were going to make to deal with Duck, I guess."

McKernan asked, "Who exactly said they were going to go after Mr. Duckett?"

"Joey said they should've done it. Jano and Bippo were hard

on Joey for not dealing with it."

"Where does Alfred Luna fit in?"

"Little Moon? I don't know exactly. They had him eavesdropping on you and had him try to intimidate me in front of the guys. I'm pretty sure he shot out the windows of my car."

"Wait, what?" McKernan said.

He explained, but said nothing about the bullet he had retrieved. "It's a distraction. He doesn't want the focus on him." Then he said, "How should I respond?"

Ward crossed his legs under the desk. "How much have you told your father?"

McKernan turned toward Mickey.

"I told him I thought it was Little Moon who shot my car. But he thinks I brought all of this on myself." He looked at McKernan. "I don't think I can count on him."

No, thought Ward, *you cannot*. "Does he know you're here?"

Mickey shook his head. "He's done with me. He threw me out."

Mike Wright chose against his son, McKernan thought. *No surprise there.*

Ward said, "You respond by doing what you usually do."

"Go to Impact?"

"The whole thing," McKernan said. "Nothing traces back to you."

"Will I have to testify in court?"

Ward said, "Let's stay in touch."

Reading her supervisor, McKernan stood. She walked Mickey toward the elevators.

"Where will you go?"

"To stay?" Mickey asked. "I have a couple of ideas."

"Maybe it's best if you avoid your father for a while. Given his relationship with DeSalvo and all."

He nodded.

"I'm sorry, Mickey. Your father...It's tough."

"No, I knew. I guess I always knew."

The elevator arrived.

"You take care, Mickey."

He gave a little wave as he stepped into the lift.

McKernan returned to Ward's office. He was standing, looking down at the traffic on McCarter Highway.

"Wire him up," she said.

He turned. "To what end? No one at Impact is speaking to him."

"Have him tell Janowitz or Bippo he overheard them."

Ward said no. "That's Newark's business. We need to know if the Teamsters sanctioned the hit. That's our charge."

"So send him to DeSalvo. Have him tell DeSalvo he heard the crew wanted to protect the local. He'll go for that."

"I don't think so. Mr. DeSalvo will react poorly if he thinks he's the subject of secrets among the members." Ward tugged down on his shirt and checked the knot in his tie. "However... Councilman Swayback might be interested in information he could leverage."

"He could do the Teamsters a favor."

Ward nodded ever so slightly.

McKernan's coffee was growing cold. "Why does Wright kick him out now? After his son's been threatened?"

"Maybe he takes it as it's a threat aimed at him, not his son."

"So what does Sgt. Wright know that requires a threat?"

New windows installed, bits of glasses vacuumed away, his possession tucked in the trunk, Mickey drove to St. Peter's and parked in the lot. He was in the hall when the clock struck and the classroom doors swung open. Debbie emerged, books in her arms; short denim skirt, no stockings, Frye boots.

"What's wrong?"

"I have to talk to you," he said.

Students walked around them.

"We'll go to the caf."

Mickey pointed down the hallway past the rows of lockers. "Let's find an empty room."

"Mickey?"

When the hall emptied, they walked toward to a classroom. Stepping inside, Mickey turned two desks to face each other, parallel to a greenboard that had been wiped clean.

"You look awful," she said, sliding her books under the desk. "Have you been crying?"

He took a breath. "Deb, I haven't been telling you the whole truth. About Impact, Duck, what I know..."

"I don't understand."

"Let me get it out," he said.

Now Debbie was crying. Mickey paced toward the window and then back across the front of the classroom.

Sniffling, she said, "So your guilt is real."

He nodded.

"Is there any reason to think he would be alive if you had told him everything?"

"I should've told him, Deb. Whether he would have been in the bar, who knows?"

"What did the FBI say?"

He said, "Do what I usually do. Go to Impact—"

"No, I mean about not telling him what you overheard."

"They didn't say. Maybe they think if they were going to kill him, they'd find him, eventually. I mean, he came to work the next day."

"Mickey..."

"Deb, I know. I should've told him."

"And everything else. The gambling, the prostitutes, the

guns. Mickey. *Mickey.*"

"I didn't want you to see me that way. I'm not—Even with all this, I'm not one of them. They wanted me to loan out money, and I said no. The Knicks tickets, I didn't use them. They invite me out, but I don't go."

"You didn't use a prostitute, did you?"

"Oh God, no." He sat across from her. "Deb, I don't gamble either. I held a gun once for about two seconds. I never hit anyone. I was around it, but I wasn't in it."

"But you protected them."

"They have a way of making you feel you're part of something ,and it takes care of you. Not everybody there is a shit, Deb, or a criminal. It's like a society."

"'A society'? How can you say that?"

"It's true. There's rules and codes and ways of behaving. You look out for each other. Even if you don't think about it, there's this little world, and you're part of it."

"But a part of what, though? Something in conflict with who you are? Something that requires you to change? It doesn't make sense."

"I see that now. I got turned around somehow. The money... I needed it to move on. And I like we can do things."

"Mickey, don't say you did this for me. Don't."

"No, no. I'm—Deb, I'm so sorry. I didn't want you to...I didn't want you not to love me."

"And you thought lying to me was the best way to do that. How could you?"

He sagged. "God, I know it sounds stupid. Everything was confused. I knew your father was right. If I wanted a future, I needed to move on. But I didn't. And then the thing with Duck. Now it's...There's nothing to hide anymore. I'm wide open over here."

They sat in silence, oblivious to passing students in the corridor, to traffic out on Montgomery Avenue.

"Say something, Deb."

"I can't make sense of it. Every night we spoke on the phone. Every weekend we were together. And you were holding this all in. You weren't true."

"No, Deb. With you, I'm me. I'm—"

"No, no. When we started, you weren't in all this. I wouldn't have fallen for you if you had been. What did you think appealed to me about you, Mickey? I mean, you dressed like the rest of us. You had that crappy Impala. We went to the movies, shared a bucket of popcorn, and hung around. Did I want a guy who made a lot of money? I didn't care about that. Mickey, you were pure. Sweet. You were honest. You went to church and you missed your Mom.

"Now who are you? Gambling, guns, gangsters. They beat a man half to death and you didn't say anything. You overheard a conversation about killing someone and you didn't call the police. Mickey, who are you?"

"Deb, please. I'm trying to amend—"

"Because you're afraid. Not because you're honorable again."

He buried his face in his hands. When he moved them away, he found Debbie starting at him, her expression severe.

"Deb, give me a chance to make it right. Please. Can't you think of it as I got a little lost somehow?"

"'A little lost'? Mickey, I'm feeling sick to my stomach. My head is spinning. You were my first. You know that. I brought you into my family. I thought we would make it. I really did."

"Deb, don't say that. Please."

She retrieved her books. "I'm sad," she told him as she stood. "I need time."

He followed her to the door. "I'll walk you—"

"No, let me go. Please."

She left the classroom and walked along the empty corridor without turning to wave goodbye.

CHAPTER NINETEEN

Mickey arrived well after the horn had sounded on the Impact dock. He went directly to the office and punched the clock. There stood Mrs. Ada with her shopping bag. She left immediately.

"I had to get my windows repaired," he said to Broadhead as he retrieved a tube from its basket.

Broadhead snorted. The *Times* crossword puzzle was on his lap.

Hobby horses to Oshawa, fuel gauges to Kitchener.

Deep in tumbledown thoughts, Mickey was unaware he had typed manifests. After tubing them out to Luna, he stood with the ochre copies in his hand as if he had no idea how they had gotten there.

Coming up on seven o'clock, the phone rang. Hope rising, he thought: Debbie. But it was Maria from Monteleone's. A water leak. They had closed early. No sandwiches tonight.

He made the long walk down the dock to take the lunch order. Hard eyes followed him as he passed waiting cargo, loaded pallets, dollies. He heard whispers, he felt sneers. As he approached Luna's booth, he looked for Jano and Bippo. They weren't there.

"No go on Monty's," Mickey told Luna. "Chicken Delight OK?"

Without facing him, Luna nodded. Then he said, "We're short two."

Not three? thought Mickey. But there was Little Moon down the line, pushing cardboard cartons on a dolly into a trailer.

He was going to say it: Benny, look at me. Why did it have to happen this way? Duck didn't tell me anything. I overheard, but I kept quiet. Why intimidate me? Why shoot my car? Why make me an enemy? I'm like you—trying to do my job, trying to get through.

But no. He was on the other side now. The Teamsters were locked and loaded here and Mickey Wright over there in his lonely place.

"Mickey," said Luna, "do what you came for, then get out."

"Benny—"

Luna turned his back.

When Mickey returned from Chicken Delight, he dropped the shopping bags and the greasy buckets of chicken on the cable reel outside Luna's shack. On the way to the office, he dodged a hand truck Caffy aimed at his shins. A rusted bolt struck him on the shoulder.

Hours later, he left without cleaning up the carbon paper.

Someone had keyed his Corolla, the paint stripped away in a jagged line along the driver's side door. His gas cap was missing.

He drove for hours. He had nowhere to go. The sky was oil black. On Route 3, he found he was heading toward Moonachie, so he turned off and wound up on Tonnelle Avenue, where his father patrolled in an unmarked car. Banging a U-turn, he went north on 95. Soon, the George Washington Bridge was in sight. Traffic was light now; he could cross easily into the Bronx where he knew no one and no one knew him.

At 4:30 a.m., he returned to New Jersey and pulled into a service area on the Turnpike. Seagulls picked at the trash scattered in the parking lot. In the men's room, he took off his T-shirt and washed vigorously, using pink hand soap from a pump. After a Styrofoam cup of coffee, he moved his car behind the brick building and changed out of his work clothes. He brushed his teeth and rinsed with 7 Up. He needed a shave, but decided against it, at least for now. Tidying his hair in the rearview mirror, he saw his eyes were red and puffy. He had cried as he circled the New York Botanical Garden, remembering Debbie had chosen it as a place to spend a Sunday: Mickey had found a spot on the street just big enough to accept his Impala. "And he has a gift for parallel parking, folks," she announced when the big car settled it. "Is there anything young Wright can't do?"

Now he drove west on Route 46. Traffic was building on the highway to the bridge. The morning sun was behind him. He clicked on the radio to find the time and discovered he would arrive well before he had to.

There were two elementary schools in the small town. In her class photo, the little girl wasn't wearing a uniform, so Mickey set up across the street from the public school's playground, first sitting behind the wheel of his scarred Corolla, then leaning against its hood. A kindly old man helped kids cross the street; they sang "Good morning, Mr. Dempsey."

Rosemary was wearing a pale-blue Kmart smock over jeans. In a pink jumper over tights, Dani skipped alongside her, holding her hand, but pulling ahead as her little friends came into view. Rosemary kissed the top of her head and, giving her a playful tap on the butt, sent her on her way.

Mickey followed his sister to the bus stop.

"Roe," he said.

She turned. "You fuck. I knew it. I knew you couldn't resist."

"Roe, please," he said, coming closer.

An old woman on the bus-stop bench put down her *Parade* and stared at them through cat's eye glasses.

"I've got no place else to go."

187

She was eager to quarrel. But she said, "What did he do?"

"Can you put me up for a while? I'll explain."

She looked down the street to see if her bus was soon to arrive. "I'll drive you."

"Yeah," she said after a moment. "OK."

She drew next to him and, as they walked toward his car, she smacked the back of his head.

"For a smart kid, you are such a dope," she told him.

Mickey had no idea where he was. "Oh shit," he said to the light-skinned black man who stood over him. "What time is it?"

"Your sister said wake you up at two. It's two. In the afternoon."

Mickey untangled himself from the crocheted throw to sit up on the sofa. Through cotton mouth, he said, "Mickey," thrusting out his hand.

"I know. Brian." He tapped the breast of his service-station shirt where it said "Carl" in red script. "Borrowed."

The living room was populated with beat-up Fisher-Price toys, nubby crayons and coloring books. There was a dent in the floor lamp's shade.

Mickey stood. "Thanks for the crash, Brian."

He was shorter than Mickey, but lean and spindly, and there was a sprinkling of gray in his Afro. "You can use the shower and there's food in the fridge. But Roe says be gone by three. That's when Dani gets home."

As he folded the throw, Mickey said, "I'd like to meet her…"

"Gone by three. You can come back after nine." Brian held out a slip of paper. "Here's the phone number. In case."

"I'm sorry about all this."

"No big thing. But, hell, I didn't even know she had a brother."

* * *

188

He told McKernan what had happened at Impact. "I don't feel safe. What should I do?"

He was in a payphone in a public park in Leonia.

She was at her desk. Minnow Duckett wasn't her only case and it required very little but to wait for Newark PD to finish with the Baldessaros, Janowitz, Bippo and Fischetti. It was a matter of time before one of them cracked: a conspiracy of five couldn't hold. Figuring the Baldessaros would stay true, if only to each other, Bonner and Corelli saw Bippo as most likely to flip. "He don't know he's a moron," said Corelli succinctly. Ward, as cautious a man as she'd ever met, wouldn't quite agree with her when she said Newark would break the case by Monday. Her thinking: The city had 170 homicides in 1973. If Newark PD knew how to do anything, it was how to work murder.

The FBI would step in when Newark retreated. She and Ward needed the Impact crew to give up DeSalvo and anyone else in the Teamsters who sanctioned the robbery and subsequent murder. Until then, she was pushing paper and waiting for a warrant to obtain the security-camera footage from a Korean greengrocer in Elizabeth who was terrified the extortion gang who beat him would return.

She looked at her watch. Ward wouldn't be back from the budget meeting until late.

"Come in," she told Mickey Wright. "We'll figure it out."

"What is it we're figuring out?" he asked.

"Come in," McKernan repeated. "We'll figure that out, too."

Now he was back in Jersey City. At Impact. He arrived along with the crew, most of whom stared at him as he rattled across the gravel to a parking space. A new gas cap was in place, but the raw scar along the side of the car remained. A guy at Pep Boys sold him a little kit and paint he called Monkey Shit Brown.

Mickey was in his Impact uniform: old T, jeans, soiled Adidas. He took his flannel shirt from the backseat, lifting it from under his textbooks. He finished off his drink as he walked toward the dock. No one said a word to him. The FBI was far away. His only weapon was an empty Yoo-Hoo bottle.

As he came up the steps, he saw Buddy Peck by the time clock. Mickey hadn't spoken to Peck since his father's wake. Last time Cheryl Peck called in looking for her husband, she and Mickey chatted, Mickey asking after the kids, Cheryl telling him she intended to return to Jersey City State—"nights, if I can get Buddy to come home on time."

"Hey Buddy."

His paperwork on the counter, Buddy Peck snarled at Mickey. "After Joey threw down for you...Fuck you, Mickey."

Prepared for resentment and hostility, Mickey met his comment without blinking, nodded his head, kept walking. His stomach was in a knot.

Mrs. Ada was at the typewriter, her paraphernalia in place.

Broadhead said, "You're to go upstairs."

Mickey went to the desk.

"Immediately."

Mickey nodded.

Louise was at the filing cabinets in a short paisley skirt, jangly belt, sandals. "Aileen Murphy," she said, pointing as if Mickey didn't know the path to Personnel.

Miglio's office was empty. The blinds were drawn.

Though she was waiting for him, Aileen Murphy seemed startled when he knocked on her door frame. She began to stand, but then remained in her chair. On her desk was a white envelope with Mickey Wright handwritten on its front.

"Have a seat, Mickey," she said.

Mickey folded his flannel across his lap. A foul odor soiled the air.

"Mickey, I'm sorry to tell you we have to let you go. I think you understand." She lifted the envelope. "This is your severance and your vacation pay."

He stood. "Should I tell Broadhead?"

"No, no. I'll call him."

Mickey thanked her.

He exited through the mechanics' bay.

Soon he was on Tonnelle Avenue with time to kill until he could return to Rosemary's.

His first free Friday night since last summer.

A fleeting thought: Maybe Debbie would welcome him if he turned up, his arrival before sunset a signal of change.

The Olsens would sit down to supper soon. Cod, buttered fingerling potatoes, green salad. The table seated four. Mickey and Debbie across from each other; Mickey peering into her dark eyes. "Mickey, stop. You're freaking me out. Look away." Mrs. Olsen is amused. "Dessert, Mickey?"

Mickey could wash up and change at a gas station. He would make himself presentable.

I've done the right thing, Deb. The slate is clean.

The slate is not clean.

Bless me, Father, for I have sinned. It doesn't matter how long it's been since my last confession: the severity of what happened in the interim can't be measured by time. Absolution is beyond your powers.

He went to the backdoor. Moths flitted around the bulb overhead. He knocked softly, not wanting to wake the little girl.

"In," said Rosemary, stepped aside.

Mickey stood next to the groaning refrigerator.

"It's not going to work," she told him.

Roe, sagging in old jeans and a T.

"No, I figured."

"You leave before Dani gets up for school. You sneak back after she's asleep, dealing with Brian. No."

She retreated to the kitchen table. A lazy Susan was populated with condiments: plastic pepper and salt shakers, store-brand ketchup, yellow mustard, salad dressing; little pink packets of Sweet'n Low. Scribbled drawings on construction paper were taped to the paneling.

Mickey sat in Brian's chair.

She said, "Thinking about what you told me. You should've gotten out of Impact, Jersey City, the whole thing. You see that, right?"

"It's easy to see it now," he told her. "Everything is beat to hell."

"Your girl. She's not going to follow."

"Debbie has it all. Family, friends, interests. Confidence. A plan. I'm the stain."

Rosemary shook her head. "You're not a stain. But you're stained. Get out while you can. Put him behind you."

"I don't—"

"Don't let him do to you what he's done to me," she said. "That son of a bitch wore me down." She twisted her fist on the table. "He ground me down."

"But you have Dani."

"You'd think that would make everything all right, wouldn't you? But I hate—I mean, I *hate*—that he's in her blood."

Sitting back, she looked into the distance as if rummaging through memories. Sighing in resignation, she said, "You're like Mom. You've got good in you. You'll make it."

He dropped his hand on her forearm. "Roe, you were magic. A big glowing firefly. 'Dancing in the Streets,' remember? The first thing I heard in the morning was you singing."

"I can't sing for shit."

He laughed. "True. But such joy, Roe."

"It's gone. And maybe that's it. I see you and I know what I lost."

"I want to us to be a family."

"You don't understand, Mickey. I could've been you. Bright, hopeful, curious. A kind heart. A future." She held up her hand.

"I'm not jealous. No. But seeing you...I know what I've lost. What that fuck took from me."

She cupped his cheek.

"You've got to go. Have your life, baby bro."

He kissed her palm.

"What sweet revenge that would be. You, Mickey Wright, happy, successful and far, far away."

"I'm not a vengeful guy, Roe."

"No, I know that. I'm just saying..." She stood slowly, as if she ached. "Kiss goodbye, Mickey."

Mickey held her. "Now the Wrights hug and kiss?"

"Forget him. Forget me. Go."

"I love you, Rosemary."

She walked past him and opened the door.

CHAPTER TWENTY

Once Mike Wright entered the Briar Rose, DeSalvo told Pug to lock the door, don't answer it for nobody. Though it was only just past nine in the morning, he knew the smelly hangdog regulars would soon arrive to begin their Saturday, elbows by the taps, nursing Schlitz, whispering grievances, settled in for hours.

With a flick of his fingers, Wright demanded a cup of coffee.

At a table next to the cigarette machine, DeSalvo was picking at a bacon-and-egg sandwich wrapped in aluminum foil. He was too agitated to eat.

Wright sat at the bar.

"Your son. Where is he?"

"No idea," Wright replied. He wore a blue suit, white shirt; his necktie was in his jacket pocket, hanging out like a tongue. Late last night, Jersey City PD hit Montgomery Gardens. One black teen killed as he tried to escape, hurdled from his vehicle as it slammed into a telephone pole. Drugs, cash and two wailing infants in soiled diapers were found. Sergeant Wright had done it again.

He said, "I kicked him out. Clothes and all."

"When we need him close, you throw him away. Genius."

Wright grimaced as he sipped the bitter coffee. "This pointing at him is bullshit. A joke. And you know it, Joe. Otherwise, you don't shoot up his fuckin' car. You put two, three in him."

Wright hadn't told DeSalvo about the spent bullet he wrestled

194

from his son. It was way too soon to play that card.

"And how do you figure you need him? The thing's fucked. You don't think Newark can tear open those mooks? They already got one Baldessaro for the truck and the merchandise. They'll give up whoever shot the shot."

"And if they don't know?"

"You're saying it wasn't them. The brothers."

"Am I saying that?" DeSalvo asked.

"It's simple then. Either Bippo or Janowitz put two from a .44 Magnum in the vic. Now, who do you know owns a .44 fuckin' Magnum?"

"A lot of people. 'Dirty Harry' is a two-hour commercial for them." DeSalvo took another bit of his sandwich and then crumbled the rest inside the foil. With no trash can in sight, he tossed the ball behind the bar. "The Feds, they threatened my nephew with some bullshit about the draft."

"So he's jammed up already. The kid deals. You're fucked, Joe."

"And you, too. You think Swayback's name don't come up? You don't think when Billy Fixx deals, he don't give up Swayback? And you, his bagman."

Wright shrugged. "I'm doing good work here, Joe. We're crushing bad guys. The newspapers—big headlines. Nobody gives a shit you threw me a couple of bottles of Scotch."

"And 100 bucks a week for you and another two for Swayback."

"Coin. Nobody cares. Meanwhile, you got a hijacking ring, you got a dead spade— " Wright stood "—and you got three Teamsters in lockup and you got your nephew's fucking gun."

"Nobody but the river got his gun."

"And once Newark is through, here comes the FBI waving the hate-crime statute, Bobby Kennedy risen from the grave. A 100 bucks a week is an issue? If I had the juice, I'd fuckin' arrest you myself. For stupidity."

DeSalvo shook his thumb toward the back room where Pug

was rattling empties. "I don't think she heard you. A little louder this time."

"Make your plans, Joe. They got your guys. The bell tolls."

"And your boy?"

"He walks. You fired him, so he walks."

DeSalvo said, "We threw him two months' pay plus vacation. Maybe he sees it as gratitude."

"Nah. You can't buy him off. He thinks he's going to heaven. Express lane."

"We want to talk to him, Mike. Tell him he ain't blamed. We just wanna know what the FBI is thinking."

Musing, Wright said, "Fuckin' kid, right? We should've left him a baker."

"We want to know what they're thinking. The Genoveses want to know."

The FBI put Mickey up at the Robert Treat, a big old slab of a hotel that, according to a yellowing card in the stationery folio, was completed in 1916 in time for Woodrow Wilson to check in. It had seen better days, but it had long served as a reliable safe house for the bureau. Up in his ninth-floor room, Mickey remembered vast ballrooms that were hosting wedding parties tonight and wondered if he could sneak down to grab a plate of hot food, maybe have someone to talk to.

McKernan told him he was to stay in his room, that only a raging fire, flames licking his door, was cause for an unapproved exit. His car was in the FBI lot below the old courthouse, a precaution to further conceal his whereabouts. McKernan delivered sandwiches and the *Star-Ledger*. Looking at his pile of textbooks and notes, she asked if he wanted her to quiz him.

"I'd like to go to Mass tomorrow," he told her.

"Not in your church, but sure."

They needed him now. If Mass made him believe he was doing

what's right, if it kept him steady, fine. A little prayer couldn't hurt.

Later, while Mickey lay on the king-sized bed, caressing the gold crucifix Debbie had given him, he heard a knock on the door. Startled, he didn't know whether to answer it. Ward had told him he was well-hidden, but he needed to watch out. A threat existed until it didn't.

"Me," said McKernan.

He wriggled back into his St. Peter's Prep T and opened the door. "Wow," said Mickey.

McKernan was in a sleeveless dress, more orange than pink, plunging neckline, short skirt, stiletto heels. Her auburn hair was lifted high, exposing a swan-like neck, and her scent reminded him of flowers after a summer rain.

"I have a date," she said, entering. "Do you mind?"

Mickey sealed the door. "Where do you keep the gun?"

She said, "You tried to call her."

"No, I—Yeah, I did. But I hung up."

That was true. The switchboard operator told McKernan the call didn't connect.

"You want her to rush over here?"

I wish, he thought.

"With a red Dodge Challenger following?"

"Are they watching her?"

McKernan said no. A guess. "We talked about this. Let it play out."

He sat on the big bed and hung his head, hands clasped between his knees. "Saturday night was our night. Of course, I'm feeling this way..."

"Give it a month. If you'd like, we'll get a message to her."

"Her father wouldn't like that," he said. Looking up, he added, "If I took finals like I was supposed to, I'd see her."

"Can't happen. You know that."

"This whole thing feels like I'm being punished for trying to do what's right."

"I'll send you up a steak," she told him. "Eat, sleep. Watch an old movie. You'll regain your perspective."

Mickey nodded as if he believed her.

"I'll be back in the morning to prep. Then we put it behind you."

Sun straining through the Sunday morning clouds, a UPS van followed Mickey's Corolla as it left St. Casmir's in the Ironbound section and turned onto McCarter Highway. Inside the van were Ward, McKernan and two surveillance specialists, Special Agents Chuck and Scavuzzo. Ward was behind the wheel.

In his Corolla, Mickey felt nothing and everything. He was at a distance from the experience yet his body tingled—McKernan and Ward role-playing it repeatedly in his hotel room, telling him what to expect and how to avoid distractions and self-recrimination, the kind that could cause him to veer from the script. "Leave the guilt here," Ward told him. "It won't do you any good."

As he drove, the van on his tail, Mickey couldn't hold a thought for a more than a few heartbeats. He was grateful he had traveled these streets many times in the old Impala his father had given him: Familiarity relieved the burden of concentration. He continued to pray.

Soon, the two-vehicle caravan crossed the Hackensack River into Jersey City, driving along not far from the Holy Name Cemetery and St. Peter's College. It proceeded to the access road to the Holland Tunnel.

Mickey tapped his turn signal and bounced into the parking lot of the All-Star Diner. As instructed, he took a spot around the side of the building. Cutting off the ignition, he saw the UPS van pass him to settle behind the diner.

Ward, in a brown UPS uniform and black boots, stepped out of the van and walked to All-Star. He told the hostess he would sit at the counter, thank you. Taking up a menu, he scanned the crowded room, peering around hustling waiters. Councilman Ed Swayback was in his customary booth in the rear corner.

McKernan leaned over and flashed the van's high beams.

Mickey left the Corolla. He walked away from it without closing the driver's side door. Realizing his error, he returned to lock it.

"You can do this," said Mickey Wright to himself.

"Yes, you can," said Nora McKernan, aware he couldn't hear her.

In the All-Star, Ward looked into the mirror behind the glassware, expecting Mickey to arrive. Instead, he saw in the reflection Joe DeSalvo of the Teamsters Local 560.

"DeSalvo's here," Ward whispered into his cuff.

"You called it," McKernan said.

Then Ward asked the man two seats down if he could borrow his *Daily News*.

"It ain't mine," said the man, who nudged it toward him.

Ward ordered coffee just as Mickey Wright came into the diner.

He couldn't help but see Ward, seated at the counter and his presence gave him a ripple of comfort. But it vanished almost instantly when he saw Swayback and, across from him, DeSalvo.

Ward stood, a copy of the *Daily News* in his hand. He walked the newspaper to the cashier. As he approached Mickey, he whispered, "Stay calm. Stick to the script."

Mickey didn't know how to respond. He reached for a mint, using the little spoon to scoop it out of the bowl.

"Your paper, ma'am," Ward said to the cashier.

Then to Mickey, he whispered, "Go on now, son."

In his flannel shirt, his St. Peter's Prep T, his jeans and soiled Adidas, Mickey headed for the rear corner.

Swayback saw him. He reached across the table and poked De-Salvo.

The councilman was wearing about the same clothes he had on the first time Mickey spoke to him: golf shirt, black slacks. Razor-cut graying hair. Cold blue eyes. Gold watch. Wedding band.

Stomach in turmoil, Mickey stood next to the booth. DeSalvo, in gray sharkskin, silver tie and Teamsters tie clasp, looked up at him with disgust.

"Can I sit?" Mickey managed.

"Scooch over, Joe," said Swayback. As the waiter approached, he held up his hand, shooing him away.

Mickey cleared his throat. "I hope—I hope you don't mind. I need to speak to you."

"Yeah. You do. You need to speak to Joe, too."

Mickey looked at DeSalvo. "He shot my car. Little Moon."

In the UPS van, McKernan let out a moan. Less than a minute in and he was freewheeling.

"You shoulda come to me," DeSalvo said. "Then all this, this mess, it goes away."

"I did come to you, Joe. And he shot my car."

"And you don't learn."

"I didn't know Duck's load was in Moonachie," Mickey said. "That's not on me. Once they found it, what could I have told you that would've helped?"

"You got cozy with the FBI." DeSalvo hissed. "We had your back. Ten-thousand—"

"Like you had Duck's?"

DeSalvo looked at Swayback. "Listen to this fuckin' wise-ass," he said. He was on edge; his bosses were displeased. They were looking hard at him.

"Mickey, what's on your mind?" Swayback said. "Get it out."

"Just tell me. My father. Was he in on it?"

"'In on' what?"

DeSalvo said, "Hold on a second. You're here to clear your old man? Are you fuckin' kidding me?"

"Joe," said Swayback. "Let him talk."

Mickey said, "I don't mean the stolen goods. The whole dock knows how that works. The stuff in our apartment tells me my father does too, so I'm guessing he knew about Moonachie. But killing Duck: Was he in on it?"

Swayback leaned in. Any trace of gentility left his expression.

In the van, McKernan said, "Hold tight, Mickey…"

"They want you to testify, don't they?" Swayback asked.

Mickey nodded. "But tell me about my father. Then I'm gone, and that's it. I won't testify. OK?"

Swayback said, "Not a great offer. You already talked, didn't you?"

"He's pulling it out of his ass, Eddie," DeSalvo said.

"I don't know how these things work," Mickey said, "but they can't force me to testify. They have no leverage. What can they take from me?"

McKernan went "whew." Speaking their language, Mickey had recited the line as written.

"Just tell me. My father…"

Swayback glanced at DeSalvo. "I've no beef with your old man. Joe?"

The union boss didn't reply. Then he said, "Dirty don't make him a killer. Not this year."

Mickey stretched out a leg and dipped his fingers into his pocket. He placed a spent bullet on the table. When DeSalvo reached for it, Mickey pushed it to Swayback.

"So you found the bullet," DeSalvo said. "I'll pay for the fuckin' windows."

"Where did you get this?" Swayback asked, examining it.

"At Impact. His nephew shot about a hundred of them into a wall. I picked it out."

DeSalvo said, "Meaning?"

"Can they match that to the bullets they took out of Duck's body?"

McKernan said, "Good…"

Swayback rattled the bullet like dice. "Let me see if I understand. If Joe drives over to Impact and he finds a hundred—"

"No," Mickey said. "I found two. The rest are gone. Swept up."

"Two," Swayback said. "Don't tell me: Your old man's got the other."

DeSalvo said, "Hold it. Who told you Duckett was shot by a .44? You don't know that."

Swayback sighed. "Let the kid talk, Joe. He wants to tell us what the FBI said, that's fine."

When the councilman caught the waiter's eye and gestured for three coffees, Mickey turned. Ward was still at the counter. He was trimming the crust off his toast.

"What I'd like to know is what the fuck he told the FBI," DeSalvo said. He leaned against the wall to face Mickey.

"I said I overheard Jano and Bippo tell Joey he should've killed Duck. But by the time I told them, Newark police had the truck and the Baldessaros. Now they have Bippo."

DeSalvo said, "No way he rolls over."

Mickey looked at him. "Bippo was born to roll over. He knows the bullets that killed Duck came from Little Moon's .44."

"Is that what the FBI told you?" Swayback asked.

"I had the impression they felt Newark had it in hand."

Before Swayback could reply, the coffee arrived. DeSalvo took the sugar shaker and sent a stream into his cup. Swayback sipped his bitter and black.

Thought Mickey, If I drink this, I'll vomit it right up…

Swayback: "What if I say 'no deal'? Just for argument's sake. What's your play?"

"I just want out, Mr. Swayback. I need to know I can go."

"And if I say no?"

In the van, McKernan said, "Do it, Mickey. Say it."

"I'm guessing you know Jano had me take Polaroids of your wife."

Swayback nodded. "Yeah. All right..."

"You had the crew beat up the guy. Your wife's guy. You had Mr. DeSalvo handle it."

Swayback glared at Mickey.

"His name. Christ Hospital knows it. Your wife knows it. My father knows it. If the press knows, you're knocked out."

Jaws clenched, temples pulsing, Swayback said, "I'm knocked out...?"

"Can you hold on to your job if the newspapers say you had this one send the crew after him? What's your value to the Teamsters if you're out of office?"

Coffee flying, silverware rattling, Swayback reached across the table and grabbed Mickey by the shirtfront. And the microphone that had been taped to his chest came loose, torn from flesh by Swayback's fist. Buttons flew as Swayback ripped open Mickey's shirt.

"Fuck," said McKernan as she threw off her headphones and leaped out of the van.

"I knew it," DeSalvo barked. "Fuckin' college boy." He pressed the nozzle of a snub-nosed revolver against Mickey's ribs. "You're going to learn what happens when you don't keep your fuckin' mouth shut. Get moving."

In retreat, Mickey slid across the booth and tumbled to the floor.

Enraged, DeSalvo leapt out after him, revolver in open view.

"FBI," yelled Ward, who had his service pistol in hand. "Drop it."

Screaming, customers dove for cover.

"DeSalvo," Ward repeated. "Drop it."

McKernan burst through the diner's doors.

"Joe," said Swayback, "what are you doing? Joe."

DeSalvo raised his gun.

Ward's shot hit him in the shoulder. He spun. Stunned, he looked at the wound, his revolver dropping to the floor.

Scrambling to stand, Mickey kicked the gun away.

Swayback sat calmly, hands on the table.

McKernan grabbed Mickey and hurried him out of the diner.

Via the microphone in his cuff, Ward summoned Chuck and Scavuzzo, who abandoned their equipment.

"I'm all right," said Mickey. But he was still trembling in the van when the Jersey City police arrived.

"Give me your keys, Mickey. We're getting you out of here."

With McKernan behind the wheel, Mickey dove into the backseat and lay flat on his stomach.

"Mickey, stick shift?" she said.

As lights flashed and whirled atop navy-and-white Furys, the Corolla lurched and exited the parking lot. Soon it was on Tonnelle Avenue and Newark bound, gears grinding until McKernan eased the transmission into third.

CHAPTER TWENTY-ONE

Mike Wright had been in a numbing sleep when the phone rang. He bumbled through jagged streams of morning light to answer it.

He jarred to full attention when the dispatcher told him, "Mike, shots fired at the All-Star. Your son—"

When Wright squealed into the diner's lot, he saw two men in suits pushing Swayback down into a black Crown Vic, a colored guy in a UPS uni supervising.

Badge in hand, Wright ran toward the ambulance.

Not Mickey on the gurney. Joe DeSalvo, blood oozing through gauze on his shoulder.

"Your son is fuckin' rat," DeSalvo spit.

The suits, the Crown Vic, the cocky colored guy—no UPS driver presses his uniform—told him it was FBI. They had Mickey, who hadn't been shot.

Motherfuckin' Mickey. You dumb, dumb son of bitch.

He was halfway to Newark when he realized the Feds weren't going to let him in to see his son and cauliflower his fuckin' ears. To see if he was all right.

The kid stands up, huh?

Stupid fuck.

Then Wright doubled back to Jersey City, where he called his union rep. He was boxed and bundled, and he knew it.

He had to get to a DA before DeSalvo did.

Then he needed the DA to carry a message to Swayback.

Your best shot, Councilman, is to keep your bagman out of it.

Deny whatever DeSalvo claims.

You do not want Sgt. Wright to respond.

Then, Councilman, you won't be implicated in Duckett's murder. Meaning no heat from the Feds. If a charge you engaged in a conspiracy to receive stolen goods sticks, remember, Councilman, every judge in the county is a Democrat just like you.

You can ride turning state's evidence against the Teamsters into the Mayor's office. The House of Representatives...

Debbie arrived early for the Astrobiology final and she was still in the hallway as her classmates arrived—all but Mickey.

Said Dr. Kinderly, "Joining us, Miss Olsen...?"

She took her seat, blue book on the desktop.

Essay: In determining a planet's potential for hosting life, what is most essential—its atmosphere, geological composition or magnetic field? Why?

Debbie down to work. Forty-five minutes later: "Time's up," Dr. Kinderly announced.

So absorbed was Debbie in the exam she hadn't thought about Mickey.

Now she wanted to see him. There was more to be said.

At her locker, she looked at the strip of photos she had taped to the door: Debbie and Mickey in the booth at Woolworth's. And there on a hook was his old hoodie, given to her for cover on a rainy day. A greeting card in which he had written a Stevie Wonder lyric: "To know the love and the beauty never known before / I'll leave it up to you to show it."

Alone in her room on last Saturday night, she realized one day she would look back and remember he had been an ideal first love. Until he wasn't. Though he had been welcomed deep into her life, he made his choice. Though is it choice if circumstance imposes the decisions? Could he ever have said no with his father on his back? In the end, where was the fault? Who was to blame?

She took down the Wilde omnibus and her notes from her locker. On Friday morning, right after the exam, she would be gone, leaving for the Jersey Shore. A new chapter, maybe. All would be as it was before she met him.

Of course it wouldn't be.

Leaving Pope Hall, she headed toward the cafeteria.

Such a trivial thing: Should I sit at our table?

As she crossed the quad, she heard a shout.

"Donna!"

Then again: "Donna!

She turned to find Mike Wright rushing toward her, his glower and frown accompanied by purposeful strides and the click-clack of his shoes. When his suit jacket fluttered, she saw his service revolver in its shoulder holster.

"Where's Mickey?" he said.

Students walked around them. Two guys in shorts, barefoot on concrete, were hurling a Frisbee.

"It's Debbie, Mr. Wright."

"Debbie," he said dismissively. "Where do I find Mickey?"

"I haven't seen him. Not since last week."

Wright shook his head in disgust.

"What's going on?" she asked.

"You seen the papers? That shootout at the All-Star Diner?"

She staggered.

"No, he's not hurt. But he's in a bind. I need to see him."

"Mickey had a gun?" It didn't seem an outlandish question. Carrying a gun would be the final step in his decline. No, using it would be, but —

"What are you talking about? No, Mickey didn't—Look, do

you know where the fuck he is or not?"

"Hey. Mouth, Mr. Wright."

"Oh, for Christ's sake. You see him, tell him don't do a god-damned thing until we talk. Tell him I'm his only hope."

She held her books against her chest. "I doubt that."

Wright choked off his response. Then he said, "Fuckin' kids."

He turned and stormed away.

The Frisbee landed at his feet. He kicked it into the bushes.

Shaking, Debbie left the quad for the newspaper honor boxes on Kennedy Boulevard, digging a dime from her purse.

Senior Special Agent Ward knocked on the hotel-room door. McKernan answered.

Mannequin neat, Ward entered. Mickey couldn't read him, but McKernan said, "Good news?"

She took the desk chair. Mickey sat on the bed.

"Newark is charging Carl Janowitz in the homicide of Minnow Duckett," he said.

"Jano?" said Mickey.

"So says Dominick Bippo. Alfred Luna confirms he gave Janowitz his .44."

"Bonner and Corelli," McKernan said. "Solid murder police."

Ward agreed.

Mickey said, "What about DeSalvo?"

"We'll see," he replied. "Janowitz can help himself."

"And what about us?" McKernan asked Ward. "Are we still on it?"

"File is with the U.S. Attorney."

"A RICO dump…"

Ward said no. "We'll get our shot." He slipped his fingers inside his suit jacket and withdrew a folded document. "Your warrant for the greengrocer's tapes."

McKernan took it and scanned the pages.

"What about my father?" Mickey asked.

Neither agent responded.

"Are you going to hassle every cop who takes stolen goods?"

Thought McKernan, *Only those who advance a criminal conspiracy and a pattern of racketeering that includes murder, extortion, embezzlement, gambling, robbery and theft.*

Finally, she replied. "One thing at a time, Mickey."

She turned to Ward and waved the warrant.

"Go," he told her.

"Mickey, I'll see you in the morning," she said as she dashed off.

Overhead, the air-conditioning wheezed.

Ward said, "We've got to plan what's next for you."

"You don't need me anymore."

Ward nodded thoughtfully. He believed the young man could be in danger. DeSalvo and his confederates needed someone to suffer. He doubted Wright would protect him, though with a father you never know.

He said, "Let's lay low until we hear what DeSalvo has to say."

His gun in my ribs. His furious nephew out on bail. Violent men on the dock. Ten-thousand strong. My own father.

"Lay low," Mickey repeated.

After a long night of watching fuzzy videotapes and drinking battery acid from Scavuzzo's Mr. Coffee, McKernan hurried home to shower and change. She arrived at the Robert Treat and rode the elevator to Mickey's room. She liked the Wright kid and appreciated the risk he took, being a dirty cop's son and all, but she wanted back in the field. As only the fifth female special agent in the bureau's nearly 40-year history, she always had something to prove. Though Ward hadn't intended to, he had defined her downward. A fair man and more willing to risk than would appear, she figured he would understand and set her free.

She knocked on Mickey's door.

She knocked again.

She put her ear to the door.

"Mickey," she said.

Now she pounded with the side of her fist.

She hurried to the phone by the elevator. As she continued to hammer the door, a manager arrived, pass key in hand.

McKernan burst in.

The bed was unmade.

His textbooks and notepads were on the nightstand.

She yanked opened the closet and the drawers. His clothes were gone.

On the desk, written on Robert Treat stationery, was a note:

"Thank you for everything. Don't worry. I'm fine.

"Goodbye,

"Mickey Wright."

CHAPTER TWENTY-TWO

In rolled-up sleeves, cargo shorts and a Baltimore Orioles cap, Mickey scanned the Belmar beach—hundreds and hundreds and hundreds of people with big colorful umbrellas, low-slung folding chairs, a tapestry of blankets, picnic baskets and sacks; portable radios issued a cacophony that couldn't compete with the roar of the pounding waves. He saw a world of its own, gleefully oblivious, not a care. On a golden late August afternoon, it seemed a kind of Eden where there were no problems that couldn't be swept aside for however long the sun continued to pour its soothing rays.

From the boardwalk's rail, his hand above his brow. Mickey saw girls in bikinis promenading at the water's edge, young teen boys tossing a football, children building sandcastles, hovering parents, women in sunhats reading magazines. Bobbing in the green-gray water, a fat man in a porkpie hat smoked a cigar. A banner trailed a prop plane: Sherry Will You Marry Me. Mickey imagined every Sherry on the Jersey shore squealing in delight and all but one soon sagging in disappointment.

He stared down at the location where so much hadn't happened for him. Throughout their last weeks together, Debbie spoke of how their summer days together would unfold. On the beach, quiet after sunset, they would unfurl a blanket in the presence of the reflections of distant stars that dotted the water:

Mickey with his hands cupped under his head, Debbie rubbing his chest around the crucifix she had given him.

"I'll count the hours, Mickey. Silly, right? I'll lay in bed and listen for your car to come up the street."

Together in the pounding waves. Together in the outdoor shower as they washed sand from their legs and feet. Together in bed, giggling as they imagined her roommates eavesdropping. Holding hands at the Sunday night barbecue, a tradition among her friends. Slow dancing at the Casino in Asbury Park. Down to Seaside Heights and its noisy playland—the big Ferris Wheel, the Swiss Bob and the Wild Mouse, Debbie squealing, the two of them kids again. "I'll win you a stuffed panda, Mickey," Debbie told him. They would eat sausage sandwiches and drink icy lemonade and be thoroughly and irretrievably in love.

Scanning, he finally found her. There was Dolores in her bikini and Alice in her Notre Dame T, both stretched out on a madras blanket. And Debbie in a turquoise one-piece, tanned, hair pulled into a ponytail, reading a paperback through sunglasses, her beach badge pinned to straw tote, feet buried in the sand, the poncho he had given her hung on her chair.

He felt a hand on his shoulder. He stiffened.

When he turned, he found a young man, tanned brown, long blonde hair that cascaded to his shoulders; a swimmer's body. His microscopic bathing suit resembled a marble sack.

"You're Mickey. I've seen your picture."

He didn't know how to reply.

"We finally meet," the man said. "I'm Brett. I took Sue's place in the house when Doyle dumped her."

Mickey believed him. "I'm not here."

"Yes, you are. I'll get her."

"Please. No."

"I know all about it. Mostly," Brett said, leaning in. "Deb and me, we talk all night."

"It's not—"

"I'll be discreet."

* * *

But he wasn't. Dolores and Alice were on their feet before Debbie pushed out of her chair. Brett pointed and they all looked. They conferred briefly and then Debbie put down her book and slipped into a T and her flip-flops. By the time she reached the boardwalk, Mickey wasn't where he had been. He was behind the wheel of a little blue hatchback. He tapped the horn and pushed open the passenger's side door.

"Can I have ten minutes?" he asked.

She sat and, hesitating, kissed his cheek.

At that moment, his heart broke again.

Soon they drove past the Shark River and onto Route 35.

"I want to apologize," he said, his eyes on the road.

"They're still looking for you. The FBI."

"Are they bothering you?"

"They're worried. But I think they believe my parents and me when we say we don't know where you are."

He said, "If they want to, they'll figure it out."

"You're in Baltimore?"

He frowned. "The cap? No, I just like the colors."

"I couldn't believe you left your Corolla."

"And the Motown tapes."

"And the tapes."

"I needed a head start. I took buses, stayed in seedy motels."

There was construction up ahead in the right lane. Mickey tapped his blinker, but had to wait for an opening.

"Your hair, the sideburns. And you lost weight."

"I'm surprised. The crap I've been eating. But you, Deb, you look fantastic. Just as I imagined it. Tell me you're having the best summer."

She hesitated. "I can't. I miss you."

"You're not dating?"

"Once or twice," she replied. "Guys are such jerks."

Mickey inched into the left lane.

"You know, we don't blame you, Mickey. My father knows you're a victim. We just don't talk about it unless it's in the papers when I call home."

Mickey looked for a place to pull over. Would they come after him if what he knew was common knowledge now? He didn't know what it would take to be forgiven. He didn't know who to ask for absolution.

At the sight of a budget motel, a little swimming pool surrounded by a parking lot, he tapped his blinker and drove behind it. He parked near tall, thick trees, remnants of a forest than had been cleared. He let the engine run and the air-conditioner sputtered.

"Mickey, no..."

"The motel? No, no." He held up his hands. "Let me get it out, OK? I practiced."

She smiled.

"I don't deserve you. Not anymore. I have to get better. I'm going to. I have a plan."

"Tell me."

"No, not now. I need to do it and I need to deserve you again. I won't ask you to wait, and I know you have your own plans. So whatever happens...The only thing I can control is getting better. To be worthy of you, Deb."

"Oh God," she said through tears. "Hold me."

When they released each other, Mickey wiped away her tears with his thumb.

"Leave me with a smile, OK?"

"Mickey, we still love each other..."

He nodded.

"Where are you going? I wouldn't tell. My hand to God, I won't."

He said no. "But you'll figure it out. Then if you want, you'll know where I'll be."

He backed the little Hornet out of the spot and drove until he found a U-turn to send them back to the beach at Belmar. He pulled in by a fire hydrant on a side street several blocks from the boardwalk.

"Mickey, one more kiss."

One more long, satisfying, heart-shattering kiss.

CHAPTER TWENTY-THREE

The routine began at 4 a.m. with Mickey unlocking the back door and entering in utter darkness. Fluorescent lights turning on with a hiss, he then tapped the coffee pot he had prepared the day before. Within twenty minutes, he had scaled the flour, measured the yeast and salt, and mixed the dough with eggs delivered daily from up in Chino. Into the spiral mixer it went. He had tweaked ever so slightly the recipe he learned at Corso's to accommodate subtle differences in the water. The old oven roared in anticipation of the first batch of what would be his pizza rounds, his most popular product. His long Italian loaves would follow.

Before sun up, two students from nearby Saddleback College arrived. Mickey loaded up the carts in front of their bicycles and off they pedaled to nearby sandwich shops and restaurants. By then, his lone full-time employee arrived. The widow Leticia Garcia had worked in the bakery in the plaza before Mickey brought it back to life. Now she handled the counter and neither she nor Mickey minded their new customers thought she was the bakery's namesake Agatha. The old customers groused about his limited menu, but his product won them over.

Stubborn and frank, the withered Mrs. Garcia prompted trust, so he would leave her in charge while he drove his Hornet to the kitchen at the Mission Viejo country club to drop off high rounds that were still warm. When he returned, he sent

Mrs. Garcia on her way. He locked the front door at 1 p.m. While he swept up, mopped, and washed down the counters, he answered the back door when his name was called and passed whatever bread remained to a driver from the mission at San Juan Capistrano. He was in his apartment by three and asleep within the half hour.

When he arrived two years ago, Mickey was surprised the summer lasted well into November. Since he slept away his afternoons, he missed some of its joys, but on the weekends, he savored the sun on the beach at Dana Point or up to Laguna where he stood in the ebbing tide and watched the surfers. In his hatchback, he kept a cooler, a sling chair, a blanket and towels, along with whatever books he borrowed from the library. He protected his head from the sun with his old Orioles cap; now and then, a baseball fan would point and give him a thumbs up.

From January into May, the weather was remarkably consistent. Rarely did it rain and a sweater was sufficient when a chill set in. He stayed close to home: Mickey's funds were low. His savings gone, what he earned went to the bank to pay off his loan with its generously low rate prompted by the community's eagerness to finance small businesses. Three nights a week, he worked the counter at a liquor store on La Paz Road. The wife of the owner took pity on the skinny *gringo* and supplied him with her leftover soups and stews. Any extra eggs delivered to the bakery found their way to his refrigerator.

He didn't mind the spartan life. The struggle helped him focus. He didn't socialize: He watched the bicentennial celebration back in New York on his little black-and-white TV. A movie matinee now and again. He was tempted to visit Disneyland, but didn't. He read more than he ever had.

Mickey had learned to suppress his curiosity. What had been was now hidden by the veil of time. Managing his memories, he could dismiss the sight of Sheila Swayback's lover bleeding and beaten on the Impact dock by conjuring up the image of his niece Dani skipping to join her friends at school. He allowed himself thoughts of his mother, who he missed dearly and whose approval he sought to regain. He no longer worried he was in danger: By applying for financing from the Union Bank of California, he understood he had put himself in a system accessible to the FBI. But they never came, never contacted him, never felt a need to issue a warning. For hours and then days at a time, he thought not at all about the Teamsters. He learned of Jimmy Hoffa's disappearance when he saw the front page of *the Orange County Register* in a trash can. Is it possible his father had protected him?

The knowledge every day brought him closer to his goal helped alleviate the often-acute pain of Debbie's absence. It was undeniable first love almost always came to an end (though the liquor store owner and his wife met in high school and were married now for 37 years). He imagined Debbie happy and that pleased him. He hadn't once taken off the crucifix she gave him.

He dared not pray for anything but the will to continue. In time, it became easier to do so. In church, he lit candles for St. Agatha and St. Honoré's, the patron saint of bakers. There were Saturday evening masses in English and Spanish.

He was not unhappy. He had gotten out.

As noon approached on a bright October day, Mickey, dressed all in white, escorted Mrs. Garcia to the sidewalk and watched as she walked with bowed legs to the bus stop in a corner of the plaza, a long loaf in her satchel. Agatha's shelves were bare—all bread sold—so he locked the door to count the bills and coins in the cash register. The bills went into his pocket, the coins into a paper bag he stored in an overhead cabinet. In the back room, he retrieved a bottle of off-brand window cleaner and a rag to wipe down the counter. When the task was completed, he went off to pick up his broom.

From a distance, he heard a knock on the front door so firm

the little bell on the frame tinkled. A student from the college applying for a position on his pre-dawn delivery team, he assumed. He put down the broom, took off his paper hat, and walked into the store.

When he looked up, he saw her.

Fumbling with the lock, Mickey shook as he opened the door.

"I figured it out," said Debbie. "Agatha's, of course. But the beach and the ocean…They're for me, aren't they?"

"Hi Deb," whispered Mickey Wright.

They fell into each other's arms.

Jim Fusilli is the author of 10 novels including *The Mayor of Polk Street*, published in 2019, and its predecessor *Narrows Gate*, which George Pelecanos called "equal parts Ellroy, Puzo and Scorsese" and *Mystery Scene* magazine said "must be ranked among the half-dozen most memorable novels about the Mob." His short fiction has been nominated for Edgar and Macavity awards.

The former Rock & Pop Critic of *The Wall Street Journal* and occasional contributor to National Public Radio's "All Things Considered," Jim is the author of *Pet Sounds*, his tribute to Brian Wilson and the Beach Boys' classic album.

For more, please see JimFusilli.com.

On the following pages are a few
more great titles from the
Down & Out Books publishing family.

For a complete list of books and to
sign up for our newsletter,
go to DownAndOutBooks.com.

The Moonlight Falcon
A Dick Moonlight PI Thriller
Vincent Zandri

Down & Out Books
November 2023
978-1-64396-344-0

Headcase Dick Moonlight PI finds himself in a world of hurt and deception when he agrees to take on a job for the Blaze Construction Company. It seems its portly, "midget" owner, Greg Blaze, believes his workers are stealing tools from him and he needs Moonlight to gather the proof.

But the more Moonlight digs into the case, the more insidious things become, including a mysterious ancient, Egyptian falcon statuette made of pure obsidian believed to be priceless that the crooked construction owner has allegedly stolen.

The Real Deal
A Duffy Mystery, 7th in Series
Tom Schreck

Down & Out Books
November 2023
978-1-64396-361-7

When Mushie, the popular street hustler of counterfeit watches, sneakers, and kitchen gadgets, comes into Duffy's bar bleeding from a gunshot wound to the stomach, Duffy and the gang are baffled. Everyone loved Mush who didn't have a mean bone in his body, Sure, he operated on the edges of what's considered proper society but, hey, so did a lot of Duffy's friends.

For Duffy, it's different. Mush was Hymie's, Duff's father-like mentor, grandson, and Duff had promised to keep an eye out for him. Now, it meant righting Mushie's wrong after his death.

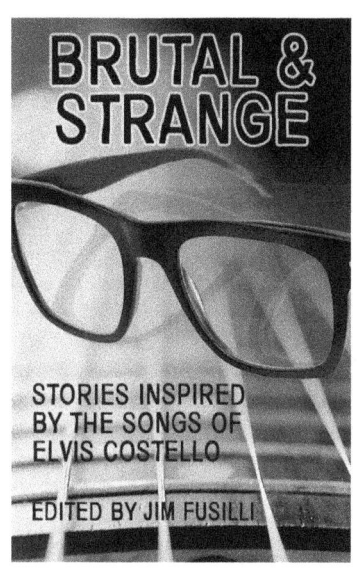

Brutal & Strange
Stories Inspired by the Songs of Elvis Costello
Edited by Jim Fusilli

Down & Out Books
December 2023
978-1-64396-345-7

In *Brutal & Strange*, edited by author and music critic Jim Fusilli, contemporary masters of crime fiction find inspiration in the compositions of Elvis Costello, who has created a surprising number of songs aren't mere nods toward unsavory events featuring questionable characters, but complete tales of murder and violence told in verse.

The marriage of Costello's themes and these award-winning authors' creativity emerge as an often-delightful and always-thrilling match.

Mickey Finn: 21st Century Noir Vol. 4
Michael Bracken, Editor

Down & Out Books
December 2023
978-1-64396-346-4

Mickey Finn: 21st Century Noir, Volume 4, the fourth volume of the hard-hitting series, is another crime-fiction cocktail that will knock readers into a literary stupor.

Contributors push hard against the boundaries of crime fiction, driving their work into places short crime fiction doesn't often go, into a world where the mean streets seem gentrified by comparison and happy endings are the exception, not the rule.

Printed in the USA
CPSIA information can be obtained
at www.ICGtesting.com
LVHW091605280424
778701LV00004B/432